The Old Formalism

The Old
FORMALISM

Character in Contemporary American Poetry

JONATHAN HOLDEN

THE UNIVERSITY OF ARKANSAS PRESS   FAYETTEVILLE 1999

03 02 01 00 99   5 4 3 2 1

Designer: Chiquita Babb

∞ The paper used in this publication meets the minimum
requirements of the American National Standard for Permanence
of Paper for Printed Library Materials Z39.48-1984.

Library of Congress Cataloging-in-Publication Data

Holden, Jonathan.
    The old formalism : character in contemporary American poetry /
Jonathan Holden.
        p.   cm.
    Includes index.
    ISBN 1-55728-568-3 (alk. paper). — ISBN 1-55728-569-1 (pbk. :
alk. paper)
    1. American poetry—20th century—History and criticism. 2. Self
in literature. 3. Character in literature. 4. Persona (Literature)
5. Literary form. 6. Ethics in literature. 7. Poetics. I. Title.
PS310.S34H65   1999
811'.50927—dc21   99-38397
                                                            CIP

For my wife, Ana,

Sine Qua Non

Acknowledgments

Wendell Berry: "The Barn" from Farming: A Handbook, published by Harcourt Brace Jovanovich, 1967.

Mark Cox: "The Blindness Desired" from Thirty-Seven Years from the Stone, by Mark Cox," 1998. Reprinted by permission of the University of Pittsburgh Press.

Dana Gioia: "Summer Storm," copyright 1995 by Dana Gioia. Reprinted by permission of the author.

Marilyn Hacker: "Villanelle," copyright © 1974 by Marilyn Hacker from Selected Poems: 1965–1990 by Marilyn Hacker. Reprinted by permission of the author and W. W. Norton & Company, Inc.

Richard Hugo: "West Marginal Way," copyright © 1961 by Richard Hugo, "Montesano Unvisited," copyright © 1969 by Richard Hugo, "Duwamish," copyright © 1961 by Richard Hugo, "The Lady in Kicking Horse Reservoir," copyright © 1973 by Richard Hugo, from Making Certain it Goes On: The Collected Poems of Richard Hugo by Richard Hugo. Reprinted by permission of W. W. Norton & Company, Inc.

Mark Jarman: "Ground Swell" from Questions for Ecclesiastes published by Story Line Press, 1997. Reprinted by permission of the author.

William Kloefkorn: "Eating Prime Rib Shortly after Being Advised to Stay the Hell away from All Red Meat," from Drinking the Tin Cup Dry (White Pine Press, 1989). Reprinted by permission of the author.

Ted Kooser: "In Late Spring," "Four Secretaries," "In Passing," and "Another Story" are from Weather Central, by Ted Kooser," 1994. Reprinted by permission of the University of Pittsburgh Press.

Peter Makuck: "Dark Preface" from The Sunken Lightship published by BOA Editions, Ltd. Reprinted by permission of the author.

Leonard Nathan: "Gap," "Meadow Foam," "Table Talk," and "Twin Snakes" are from *Carrying On: New and Selected Poems,* by Leonard Nathan," 1994. Reprinted by permission of the University of Pittsburgh Press.

Naomi Shihab Nye: "Arabic Coffee," reprinted by permission of the author, 1999.

Hilda Raz: "Isaac Stern's Performance," "Vowels," "Mu," and "Petting the Scar" from *Divine Honors*" by Hilda Raz, Wesleyan University Press by permission of University Press of New England.

William Stafford: "Evening News," "Deerslayer's Campfire Talk," "Shadows," "Behind the Falls," "This Book," "Mornings," and "For the Governor," Reprinted by permission of The Estate of William Stafford.

David St. John: The passage from "Hush" appears in *Study for the World's Body: New and Selected Poems* (HarperCollins, 1994), by David St. John." 1994, David St. John. Reprinted by permission of the author.

William Trowbridge: "Enter Dark Stranger" and "Kong Looks Back on His Tryout with the Bears" from *Enter Dark Stranger,* copyright © 1989 by William Trowbridge. Reprinted by permission of the University of Arkansas Press.

Bruce Weigl: "The Impossible," originally published in *The American Poetry Review,* and subsequently collected in *What Saves Us* (TriQuarterly Books/Northwestern University Press, 1992). Reprinted by permission of the author.

Richard Wilbur: "Mind" from *Things of this World,* copyright of " 1956 and renewed 1984 by Richard Wilbur, reprinted by permission of Harcourt, Inc.

Paul Zimmer: "Zimmer Envying Elephants" from *Family Reunion: Selected and New Poems,* by Paul Zimmer," 1983. Reprinted by permission of the University of Pittsburgh Press.

Contents

Introduction

Poets are athletes of the mind; but the performances they put on do not take place in stadiums or on television. The performances take place in books, and the quality of the performance depends almost wholly upon the existence of an educated and willing reader; for the art of poetry is preeminently an art of reading.

A lovely little poem about the contract between writer and reader is the poem "This Book," by William Stafford. "This Book" is the prefatory poem for his most political collection, *Allegiances,* published by Harper and Row at the height of the Vietnam War. Although the poem does not say so explicitly, it presents reading as a political act. The speaker is a book.

> Late, at the beginning of cold,
> you push your breath toward home.
> Silence waits at the door.
> You stamp, go in, start the fire—
> from any part of the room I suddenly say
> "Hello," but do not get in your way.
>
> Quiet as all books, I wait, and promise
> we'll watch the night: you turn a page;
> winter misses a stride. You see
> the reason for time, for everything in the sky.
> And into your eyes I climb, on the strongest
> thread in the world, weaving the dark and the cold.

The poem envisions what I think of as both the ideal reading situation for poetry and the ideal use for it—as a source of sustenance for an alienated citizen who finds himself like a foreign traveler in his own country. He returns home to a book. It is like finding a bottle of fresh milk left in the refrigerator. Gratefully, he drinks. But what he imbibes is something less palpable than milk: words.

In its historical context, with its political title, *Allegiances* reminds me strongly of Jacques Prevert's book *Paroles* (1945), with its double entendre: *paroles* means also *passwords*. It reminds me also of Adrienne Rich's *Leaflets* (1969), a book published in the year before *Allegiances* but in the same dire climate. On page 58 of *Allegiances*, in the poem "Evening News," Stafford presents the immediate historical context of the book:

> That one great window puts forth
> its own scene, the whole world
> alive in glass. In it a war happens
> only an eighth of an inch thick.
> Some of our friends have leaped
> through, disappeared, become unknown
> voices and rumors of crowds.
>
> In our thick house every evening
> I turn from that world,
> and room by room I walk, to
> enjoy space. At the sink I start
> a faucet; water from far is
> immediate on my hand. I open our
> door, to check where we live.
> In the yard I pray birds,
> wind, unscheduled grass,
> that they please help to make
> everything go deep again.

What kind of athlete was William Stafford? A runner, a message carrier like Paul Revere, carrying messages that, though in plain-enough-sounding language, are in a code; for as with all achieved poetry Stafford's poems, despite his well-known disclaimers to the contrary, assume a reader who is an initiate. His poem "This Book" is a kind of whispered password, a secret handshake and wink, a welcoming "home." Such is the "ground" (to borrow the word made so fashionable by Martin Heidegger) on which these essays are founded: a set of assumptions about the aesthetic and social uses of poetry. The assumptions are traditionalist.

"Evening News" is against television. For Stafford, the most reliable source of truth is experience lived and then tested and confirmed in books. It is, for me, too. I was raised among books, by a hyperintellectual father, a physical chemist who was something of a polymath. He had read T. S. Eliot. He was a pianist. He was a mathematician. He was a carpenter.

I learned to revere books and to regard the world's most successful intellectuals, such as J. Robert Oppenheimer and Ludwig Wittgenstein, with awe. Such awe influences the way I approach poetry. I approach it eagerly, as a devoted fan. I unashamedly romanticize the figure of the poet, male or female, and my first impulse is to go along with the poet, to accept who the persona appears to be, just as when, reading a short story, I believe in the fictional world presented on the page as I do the scenes on a movie screen. I am not just willing to "suspend disbelief." I am *unusually* willing. I am not naive. I am artfully naive. My reaction to poems that I like is simply to point to them. *There: truth that is its own testimony.* Hence, my reaction to achieved poems is not very analytical.

The way I discuss poems is simple. I try to notice what is there the way I might if I were studying botany, hope to notice the features of a plant and its immediate environment. But what I am most eager to notice is its beauty, in terms of form and content, which I termed two books ago its "style" and its "authenticity."

Poetry is more than ever under siege on all sides, not only by the seductions of media but by a dwindling culture of readers, "logocentrists," according to the Theorists (many of whom are enemies of the art of poetry). Indeed, as Pound had told us in "Mauberly," American culture has always been intrinsically inimical to poetry. But now, in the late nineties, it becomes apparent that this culture is the enemy of *all* reading. Stafford—a prophet and a genius—was poignantly, terribly aware of this before almost anybody else. In his little memoir, *Down in My Heart*, about his experiences as a conscientious objector during World War II, he wrote:

When are men dangerous? We sat in the sun near the depot on Sunday afternoon in McNeil, Arkansas, and talked cordially with some of the men who were loafing around in the Sabbath calm. Bob was painting a watercolor picture; George was scribbling a poem in his tablet; I was reading off and on in *Leaves of Grass* and enjoying the scene. . . . It was March 22, 1942. . . .

I looked up. The onlooker, a handsome young man, well-dressed, . . . had snatched George's poem and was reading it.

"What's the idea of writing things like this?" he challenged. "If you don't like the town, you haven't any right to come around here." I was familiar with the edge of his voice. He knew we were CO's. . . .

The young man spoke, not directly to us but to the other townsmen, some of whom had drawn nearer, about our being CO's. There was more muttering, in which we began to hear the quickening words—"yellow" and "damn." At first these words the men said, about us, to each other; then the faces were turned more our way when the words were said. A short, strong man broke into action, went to where Bob was still sitting, and grabbed the drawing board.

There are three possible responses to what I've called the "siege." One would be to join the naysayers and, like Joseph Epstein in his infamous essay *Who Killed Poetry*, to add one's voice to the collective moan. A second response would be revolutionary, to propose an alternative aesthetic, one presumably more "in key" with its "time." To adopt this alternative would be naive: aesthetic revolution has been attempted too many times to mention. Modernism was such an attempt. All it did was promote an elitist mode of poetry even more out of key with its time than before. A third response—a counterrevolutionary one—would be more modest. It would be to continue and to modify the original reaction to the high modernist doctrine of impersonality, signaled by the advent of so-called confessional poetry in 1959, with publication of Robert Lowell's *Life Studies* and picked up on by Anne Sexton, Sylvia Plath, and W. D. Snodgrass. At last, poets had permission to write a poetry out of their own personal experience again, to employ the first-person singular pronoun "I." The suicides of such writers as Sylvia Plath, Anne Sexton, and Randall Jarrell, however, sounded a note of warning. Authenticity—nakedly autobiographical poetry—could be dangerous to write. When the persona—the "I" of a poem—is a close version of the author, the emotional investment that the poet makes in his or her poem is extreme enough that a poet has to be careful what to say.

The most logical way around this danger—the safest—would be to deploy a *fictional* first-person pronoun, as in a dramatic monologue or, if the identity of the speaker is not as historically specific as in, say, Robert Browning's "My Last Duchess," to write a "persona" poem. Many poets, when writing in the first person singular, have done this; but the results can be problematical. Consider, for example, Bruce Weigl's well-known poem "The Impossible":

> Winter's last rain and a light I don't recognize
> through the trees and I come back in my mind
> to the man who made me suck his cock
> when I was seven, in the sunlight, between boxcars.
> I thought I could leave him standing there
> in the years, half smile on his lips,
> small hands curled into small fists,
> but after he finished, he held my hand in his
> as if astonished, until the houses were visible
> just beyond the railyard. He held my hand
> but before that he slapped me hard on the face
> when I would not open my mouth for him.
>
> I do not want to say his whole hips
> slammed into me, but they did, and a black wave
> washed over my brain, changing me
> so I could not move among my people in the old way.
> On my way home I stopped in the churchyard
> to try and find a way to stay alive.
> In the branches a redwing flitted, warning me.
> In the rectory, Father prepared

the body and blood for mass
but God could not save me from a mouthful of cum.
That afternoon some lives turned from the light.
He taught me how to move my tongue around.
In his hands he held my head like a lover.
Say it clearly and you make it beautiful, no matter what.

Although the events related so clearly in the poem above could have happened to Weigl, my sense is that they are made up. Particularly suspect to me is the line "He taught me how to move my tongue around." Possibly the poem is a composite of sexual details from various heterosexual episodes; what "authenticity" it exhibits would spring from those. The question of authenticity is rendered still more problematical by the five-page essay in the fall 1996 *Poetry East*, where Weigl himself has written about the origin of "The Impossible":

For fifteen years I had been writing poems about the American war in Vietnam and its consequences as I had felt and witnessed them. Although during that time I wrote more poems about subjects not directly representational of the war, the war seemed to penetrate everything I wrote. . . .

Looking at my poem again, long after the fact of its many drafts through many years, I can see that I was struggling to find a balance between the two stanzas and the change of consciousness their juxtaposition represents. After the slap, there's a break because that's where the change takes place, where a new order begins. First there is resistance, and then there is that break accentuated by the slap, and then everything changes. Man to man, a slap is an insult, but here the slap means *snap out of it* or *snap into this*. The boy is slapped out of one realm and into another. . . .

Perhaps most problematic in the poem for me as the poet, and for many readers as well, it seems, is the gentleness that accompanies my rendering of the attacker. The moment of that gentleness is the great mystery of the poem to me, and probably the single most important thing that allowed me to write this poem in the first place. The world becomes visible in an almost ethereal way after the essential moment of the poem, as though the boy's senses are muted by the act of the forced fellatio. When one is traumatized, the world recedes, and when the trauma stops, the world gradually returns, only things are different. I thought I could leave him there in the years, but I kept seeing that half smile, and his small hands, and I kept feeling his slap across my face. Quiet forces of violence dismantled the hamlet of my boyhood. That first slap led to others, and, somehow those other slaps led me to the war.

The paradox of my pathology as a writer is that the war ruined my life and in return gave me art. . . . When I looked back and found that man in the railyard, his cock glistening in his hand, I saw him from the point of view the war had forced me to assume, so I was not afraid to say the thing clearly.

My guess is that Bruce Weigl, as he sought to find an objective correlative to what the war did to him, invented this—the most disgusting and irreversible initiation that he could. I know Bruce. I could ask him. But I won't. I shouldn't have to. Reading "naively," I should either accept the poem and wince or, if I reject it, reject out of disillusionment—by being unable to suspend disbelief.

A less drastic situation is proposed in William Stafford's most famous poem, "Traveling through the Dark," a poem based on fact:

> Traveling through the dark I found a deer
> dead on the edge of the Wilson River Road.
> It is usually best to roll them into the canyon:
> that road is narrow; to swerve might make more dead.
>
> By glow of the tail-light I stumbled back of the car
> and stood by the heap, a doe, a recent killing;
> she had stiffened already, almost cold.
> I dragged her off; she was large in the belly.
>
> My fingers touching her side brought me the reason—
> her side was warm; her fawn lay there waiting,
> alive, still, never to be born.
> Beside that mountain road I hesitated.

Imagine my confusion when an acquaintance of mine, Norbert

Hirschhorn—a world-renowned researcher and the man who invented the process of "rehydration" of cholera victims—declared to me that the fawn couldn't have been alive. The fetus would die the instant the mother did. Hirschhorn declared that he would never believe another word of Stafford. I could not persuade him to accept the poem as what Stafford *thought* he remembered. But one of the reasons why Stafford is so widely admired is precisely *because* he remembered it that way. It was part of his character. Rather, it was part of the character of his persona in this poem. In first-person singular poems, unless specific instructions to the contrary are given, the convention is to consider them—the author and the persona—as the same.

It is inevitable, particularly since the late fifties with the publication of Allen Ginsberg's "Howl" and Robert Lowell's *Life Studies*, when the personalization of American poetry was permitted, that our evaluation of a poet's work should involve not only an assessment of his or her technical skill as an artist, but also an assessment of the poet's character. Perhaps the most important treatise on this subject is the passionately argued tract *On Moral Fiction*, by John Gardner, published in 1978. Gardner writes:

> My basic message throughout this book is as old as the hills, drawn from Homer, Plato, Aristotle, Dante, and the rest, and standard in Western civilization down through the eighteenth century; one would think all critics and artists should be thoroughly familiar with it, and perhaps many are But my experience is that in university lecture halls, or in kitchens at midnight, after parties, the traditional view of art strikes most people as strange news.
>
> The traditional view is that true art is moral: It seeks to improve life, not debase it. It seeks to hold off, at least for a little while, the twilight of the gods and us.

There is, then, in addition to the theme of *reading*—poetry as an art of reading—the theme of character: the character of the persona of a poem. How has the poet chosen to present him- or herself to the world? Why?

Does evaluation of the persona's character fit in the critical enterprise? Where? Having watched on television the abuses of authenticity—people confessing on Geraldo Rivera, the lady at Stanford confessing to her incestuous affair with her father—one might wonder about the value of "authenticity." What is the difference between first-person-singular poetry and therapy? This book does not attempt any direct answers to such questions. It seeks, instead, to provoke by means of examples, by approaching poems "naively" and reading them closely in an old-fashioned, new-critical way, but with this difference.

The new-critical, "scientific" method of reading, conceived in the spell of T. S. Eliot's theory of impersonality, was Eliot's attempt, for reasons which we now know were defensive, to keep the threat of autobiography out of poetry. It succeeded. But issues regarding the character of the poet—his or her moral authority—tended to be neglected. There was plenty of good reason for this. As somebody close to the poetry world, Po-Biz, I am painfully aware of the amoral behaviors of many poets. Perhaps the most harrowing book about this, *Secret Life*, was published in 1995 by the poet Michael Ryan. The book documents how he was fired from Princeton University for sexual addiction.

The character of the poet is a topic we still shy away from. But it is an unavoidable topic. Though I think that it would be unwise for me—for anybody—to attempt a systematic treatise on this issue, it is the implicit theme of all the chapters that follow, beginning with "Character in Contemporary American Poetry"—an inquiry into the moral authority of contemporary American poetry, a moral authority which, because this poetry is preeminently a personal poetry, immediately inquires into the moral authority of the poet, or his or her representative.

In part 1, "The Practice," I begin with what is perhaps the most important essay in this book, "Character in Contemporary American Poetry," where I consider "character" in the light of Aristotle's *Rhetoric* and in the light of C. S. Lewis's chapter on Satan in *Preface to Paradise Lost*. Next, in "American Male Poetry of Sensibility," I turn my attention to considering "styles" of the poetic persona, its frequent narcissism. In "Character Weakness: *Mauvaise Foi*," I discuss the Michael Ryan case and its cultural implications in the late nineties. In "Sex and Poetry" I consider questions of epistemology and decorum: the difficulty which a poet faces when trying to render immediate experience in poetry, particularly the life of the body. "Rhetoricity" analyzes fashion in the formulas for figurative language and various issues regarding poetic convention. "The Public Nature of End-Rhymed Poems" demonstrates how, generally, the methods of *inventio* employed by contemporary practitioners of free verse—free association—foster a more subjective and perhaps a more subversive vision than is found in the best contemporary end-rhymed poems, which, as has been often charged, *do* enforce a more polite decorum. Finally, "The Old Formalism" demonstrates how so-called free verse is really a medley of traditional prosodies, how free verse can best be scanned, and how there seems to be an inherent trade-off between metaphorical richness and prosodic richness in poetry. This essay leads naturally to part 2, "Personae," in which I pay close attention to ten different personae: Leonard Nathan, Ted Kooser, Richard Hugo, Paul Zimmer, Bill Kloefkorn, William Trowbridge, Jack Myers, William Stafford, Mary Kinzie, and Hilda Raz. All of them have either been significantly misunderstood, neglected, or both.

But always I return to the Poem—to particular poems—believing that, as Louis Simpson put it in his famous 1984 lecture at the University of Alabama, "The Character of the Poet":

> Those who have no great liking for poetry like to explain it. The poets have been willing to see this happen—they are workers and not given to abstract thinking. They believe that the best literary criticism and the only kind that's likely to last is a poem.

I

THE PRACTICE

Character in Contemporary American Poetry

IN ARISTOTLE S TREATISE on rhetoric, much attention is devoted to considerations of *ethos*, a term which in Lane Cooper's 1932 translation is roughly the equivalent of *character*. On page 8, we read:

> Of the means of persuasion supplied by the speech itself there are three kinds. The first kind resides in the character [ethos] of the speaker; . . . The character of the speaker is a cause of persuasion when the speech is so uttered as to make him worthy of belief; for as a rule we trust men of probity more, and more quickly, about things in general, while on points outside the realm of exact knowledge, where opinion is divided, we trust them absolutely. This trust, however, should be created by the speech itself, and not left to depend upon an antecedent impression that the speaker is this or that kind of man.

On page 46, ethos is elaborated further: "Character is manifested in choice [in what men choose to do or avoid]; and choice is related to the aim or end." This seems to amend the first passage, to assert that it is what a person does which shows his character, not necessarily what he says (however skillfully).

In America in the late nineties, Aristotle sounds more convincing than ever, but more problematical, too. About image making—the manufacture of "an antecedent impression that the speaker is this or that kind of man"—we know much more than Aristotle, enough to be radically skeptical of any and every such impression. With the perfection of "digital retouching," not even photographs—once the standard journalistic touchstone of historical truth—can be trusted.

3

When we are considering poetry, especially the dramatic lyric, considerations of ethos are even more problematical; for the conventional way of reading a poem such as, say, Robert Frost's sonnet "Design," links the pronoun "I" to the author, raising the question, whose ethos are we considering when we read a poem? Is it that of the author? Or is it that of a fictional character—the "persona"? Are we deducing this persona's ethos from a single poem or from a wider context? How much do considerations from outside the poem influence our judgment of the author/persona's ethos?

Frost, for all his avuncular folksiness in poems like "Mending Wall," was reputedly a vain and highly competitive man. In private he was not nice. How much of our admiration of the persona's ethos in the poems of the late William Stafford is connected to our knowledge that he was a conscientious objector during World War II? How much of our admiration of the persona's ethos in the poems of the late Theodore Roethke is modified by our knowledge that he was manic-depressive? These questions are radically compounded when we consider the *performance* of poetry, when the physical appearance of poets plays a significant role in their ethos. Beautiful people tend to look intelligent and compassionate. Ugly people don't. Old people tend to look wise and experienced. Young people tend to look full of ardor. I think of the many poets that I have seen performing, most of whom I know personally. The power of a reading is so radically influenced by the physical presence of a poet that, once one has seen it, it is impossible to disentangle the quality of a poet's poem from the quality of her looks and from the memory of her voice. Indeed, as James Hillman argues brilliantly in his book *The Soul's Code: In Search of Character and Calling*:

> When you look at a face before you, . . . you see a whole gestalt. All the parts present themselves simultaneously. . . . You are born with character. . . . The very word "character" originally meant a marking instrument that cuts indelible lines and leaves traces. And "style" comes from *stilus* (Latin), a sharp instrument for incising characters (for instance, letters). No wonder style reveals character and is so hard to change.

What Hillman is proposing here is that we can get an intimation of a person's character from her face as well as from her literary style. It's a pleasing notion. If only life were that simple: evil people looked evil; good people looked good. But I would prefer, if possible, to consider poems as if we did not know their authors personally and had never seen them in person; for the test of the ethos of a poetic persona is whether it can rely entirely on *verbal* means of persuasion. The ideal reading situation, as I have proposed at the outset of this book, envisages a reader alone with the voice of a book.

I will present to you, then, three salient examples of ethos in poems. The first is the poem "Malebolge," by the poet Fred Marchant, in which he describes how, having enlisted in the Marines, he decided to become a C.O. The poem is set in Okinawa.

> In my room, hands behind
> my head, I am deciding
> to quit the Marine Corps as a conscientious objector.
>
> *Nei-San* is how it might be spelled phonetically.
> Sister or Miss
> in Japanese, but we use it for the Okinawan maids.
> My roommate has
> what is called a "ranch" and spends his weekends
> with our *Nei-San*
> in a house outside the gate. How easily we all take
> to the minor pleasures
> of empire: *Nei-Sans* to brasso our belt buckles, . . .

In the poem's third stanza, Marchant recounts a vision of himself in a war, of combat as a classical test of manhood, and then comes one of the most visionary passages of poetry that I have ever encountered. Marchant escorts the reader through hell and back—death and rebirth:

> The strangest moment in the Inferno: when Dante's arms
> are wrapped around
> the shoulders of Virgil, who is himself climbing down
> the coarse-haired flank

Character in Contemporary American Poetry

of Satan, whose enormous body is locked in a lake of ice.
    Suddenly Virgil seems
to be climbing back up, and Dante is bewildered,
    terrified as a child,
and needs to be told they have just passed through
    the core of the fallen
world and they are now hand over hand on their way
    to the earth's other side.

Seven lines later, Marchant describes the process leading to his ultimate decision to renounce war.

in a white blockhouse, on a spartan
    single bed, in skivvies
and flip-flops, I ask myself again what *would* I
    be willing to trade,
what part of my body, how much of my life would I pay
    for one poem, one true
line about the war. Then a voice not quite my own,
    but close to my face
and as if behind a wire mesh wonders just how grand
    how filled with epiphany
the poem would have to be if the cost was an arm or more
    belonging to another?

It's perhaps useful to point out that Marchant is linking certain types of rhetoric—those that are "grand/ . . . filled with epiphany"—to injuring others and to self-display. He is worrying about whether it is possible to write great poetry without showing off. The answer is yes. Indeed, he has already shown the answer to us in his paraphrase of the passage in Dante. We wince at the paradox: that in order to present himself or herself as authentically "good," a poet must not only appear to be motivated by something other than self-interest. He or she must *be* authentically "good." Try as many writers do, ethos cannot be successfully faked.

Another convincing poem of ethos is "Arabic Coffee," by Naomi Shihab Nye. Like every achieved poem of ethos, it has a didactic quality that is neither preachy nor offensive, combined with a testimonial quality.

It was never too strong for us:
make it blacker, Papa,
thick in the bottom,
tell again how the years will gather
in small white cups,
how luck lives in a spot of grounds.

Leaning over the stove, he let it
boil to the top, and down again.
Two times. No sugar in his pot.
And the place where men and women
break off from one another
was not present in that room.
The hundred disappointments,
fire swallowing olive-wood beads
at the warehouse, and the dreams
tucked like pocket handkerchiefs
into each day, took their places
on the table, near the half-empty
dish of corn. And none was
more important than the others,
and all were guests. When
he carried the tray into the room,
high and balanced in his hands,
it was an offering to all of them,
stay, be seated, follow the talk
wherever it goes. The coffee was
the center of the flower.
Like clothes on a line saying
You will live long enough to wear me,
a motion of faith. There is this,
and there is more.

The achieved poem of ethos will affirm love in spite of "the hundred disappointments." It will be oriented to the future. It will risk sentimentality but overcome it. Most significant, it will be generous, focused not on the poet's self but on other people.

Naomi Nye's poem suggests that a primary element of human

goodness is attentiveness to others. What about evil? The most plausible description of it that I have ever read is in Milton's *Paradise Lost*. C. S. Lewis in the Ballard Matthews Lectures delivered at University College, North Wales, in 1941, and published by Oxford University Press in 1942 as *Preface to Paradise Lost*, in the chapter on Satan, describes it beautifully. Why did Satan try to lead a rebellion against Messiah?

> On his own showing, he is suffering from a "sense of injured merit" (I, 98). This is a well-known state of mind, which we can all study in domestic animals, children, film-stars, politicians, or minor poets; and perhaps nearer home. Many critics have a curious partiality for it in literature, but I do not know that anyone admires it in life. When it appears, unable to hurt, in a jealous dog or a spoiled child, it is usually laughed at. When it appears armed with the force of millions on the political stage, it escapes ridicule only by being more mischievous. And the cause from which the Sense of Injured Merit arose in Satan's mind—once more I follow Mr. Williams—is also clear. "He thought himself impaired" (V, 662). He thought himself impaired because Messiah had been pronounced Head of the Angels. . . . No one had in fact done anything to Satan; he was not overtasked, nor removed from his place, nor shunned, nor hated—he only thought himself impaired. In the midst of a world of light and love, of song and feast and dance, he could think of nothing more interesting than his own prestige.

Lewis goes on to marvel at Satan's ability not merely to lie to others but to deceive himself:

> What we see in Satan is the horrible co-existence of a subtle and incessant intellectual activity with an incapacity to understand anything. This doom he has brought upon himself; in order to avoid seeing one thing he has, almost voluntarily, incapacitated himself from seeing at all.

"Almost voluntarily": Lewis is describing, in his own literary terms, the nature of what, in Sartre's *L'Etre Et Le Neant* is called *mauvaise foi*. In a passage of epic comedy, Lewis describes Satan in the following catalog:

Now listen to Satan: In Book I at line 83 he starts to address Beelze-bub; but in line 94 he is stating his own position. . . . He meets Sin—and states his position. He sees the Sun; it makes him think of his position. He spies on the human lovers; and states his position. In Book IX he journeys round the whole earth; it reminds him of his own position. . . . Satan has been in the Heaven of Heavens and in the abyss of Hell, and surveyed all that lies between them, and in that whole immensity has found only one thing that interests Satan.

Imaginative literature requires conflict. Fred Marchant's "Malebolge" is grounded in conflict. Nye's beautiful "Arabic Coffee" is grounded in conflict, "the place where men and women / break off from one another." Sentimentality—the enemy of literature—is praise without conflict. In order not to lapse into sentimentality, does poetry then have to always be about war or where "men and women / break off from one another"? No. Most of the occasions in which the operation of "goodness" in human affairs (and, on rare occasions, in poetry) may be observed are far more quotidian. Consider, for example, the following poem by Peter Makuck:

Dark Preface

The blind—
They're barely noticed
Unless, as today, I see one
Nearly hit by a car; he freezes, then moves again,
A kind of sleep stumble, following secret
Footage in the skull. His cane whispers
Through leaves on the walk—whispers
I follow at a distance, almost afraid
Of the eyepits, the face tilted back
As if searching
For something gone from the sky.
He shuffles past deafening rock and the blank
Of frat house windows.

On a dark street, I watch him disappear
Into a darkened house,
The light unexpected

Yellow as forsythia
That borders my parents' back porch
Where my deaf cousin and his signing friends
Are waiting for beer.
I pause at the door.
Delight creases their cheeks.
Words fill the eyes. Hands
Ballet; fingers fold and open, circle,
Figure the air and make it mean
Something funny this time. They laugh
A laughter so pure, you're listening
To nothing but light.

This beautiful poem requires perhaps less paraphrase than the Marchant or the Nye poems. Like the other two poems, it is a humble poem. The poet does not call attention to himself. We experience the benignity of the author's personal ethos not because he chooses to tell us about it. His goodness arrives to us, as it were, by accident—unguided. But, like all good poems, "Dark Preface" notices its own noticing, and this lends it (though inadvertently) a faintly didactic quality: the poem is, to some extent, *about* noticing. The blind are "barely noticed / unless . . . I see one / Nearly hit by a car." From then on, Makuck notices the way they walk, "A kind of sleep stumble," and begins imaginatively to put himself in their places until, at the end of the poem, his identification is limited by his ignorance of sign language. All that he can infer is that apparently the cousin or one of the cousin's friends has signed a joke to the others. What is especially significant to me is that Makuck imaginatively puts himself in the place of others. He didn't have to. I repeat: *He didn't have to.* Makuck's vision has this mysterious, "adventitious" quality. It is voluntary. Attention given voluntarily (as all children know) is love.

Goodness—personal ethos—is voluntary. Therefore it is groundless. To some, it may seem to be adventitious. It is a mystery. Most people's reaction to goodness in other people is to be agreeably surprised, then simply grateful. On the other hand, as Lewis wrote, we understand all too well the motives of people who are bad.

> In all but a few writers, the "good" characters are the least successful . . . To make a character worse than oneself it is only necessary to release imaginatively from control some of the bad passions which, in real life, are always straining on the leash; the Satan, the Iago, the Becky Sharp, within each of us, is always there and only too ready, the moment the leash is slipped, to come out . . . But the real high virtues which we do not possess at all, we cannot depict except in a purely external fashion. We do not really know what it feels like to be a man much better than ourselves. . . . Heaven understands Hell and Hell does not understand Heaven.

Occasionally (but only occasionally) we see this in literature: in Billy Budd, it is the inexplicable virtue of the character Billy Budd that drives Claggart insane with jealousy. Billy Budd does not understand why he is being persecuted.

James Hillman, in The Soul's Code, links ethos to what he calls the daimon:

> In the beginning, even before Socrates and Plato, was Heraclitus. His three little words "Ethos anthropoi daimon," frequently rendered as "Character is Fate," have been quoted again and again for twenty-five hundred years. No one can know what he meant, though few fail to offer interpretations, as this list of English translations demonstrates:
>
> > "Man's character is his Genius."
> > "Man's character is his daimon."
> > . . .
> > "Character is fate."
>
> . . . What about ethos, the first term of Heraclitus' fragment? To our ears, it sounds like "ethics." This loads ethos, a Greek word unencumbered by piousness, with all the moralism of Hebrew, Roman, and Christian religiosity. If we try to strip away the ethics from ethos, we find that it carries more the meaning of "habit."

"Habit." How Aristotelian Hillman sounds. We recall Aristotle's disappointingly banal definition of Art: *Habit of production according to right method.* Is Character, good or bad, an art? C. S. Lewis's *Preface*, though written in 1941, contains moral advice for contemporary writers. Lewis laments, rather sadly, "the decline in Milton's fame," a decline which "marks a stage in the rebellion of 'civilization' against civility."

> A much more respectable class of readers dislike it because they are in the grip of a particular kind of realism. Such people think that to organize elementary passions into sentiments is simply to tell lies about them. The mere stream of consciousness is for them the reality, and it is the special function of poetry to remove the elaborations of civility and get at "life" in the raw. Hence (in part) the popularity of such a work as *Ulysses.* In my opinion this whole type of criticism is based on an error. The disorganized consciousness which it regards as specially real is in fact highly artificial. It is discovered by introspection —that is by artificially suspending all the normal and outgoing activities of the mind and then attending to what is left. In that residuum it discovers no concentrated will, no logical thought, no morals, no stable sentiments, and (in a word) no mental hierarchy. Of course not; for we have deliberately stopped all these things in order to introspect.

Introspection is a habit that can be cultivated by "suspending all the normal and outgoing activities of the mind and then attending to what is left," in Coleridgian terms, by "a willing suspension of disbelief." It is an art. Character, good or bad, introspective or generous, is an art. It is something one works on. Bad people work at being bad. They practice it.

In *Paradise Lost,* Book IX, in Satan's speech, we watch it being used for evil as Satan tempts Eve. He flatters her extravagantly, daintily:

> Wonder not, sovran Mistress, if perhaps
> Thou canst, who are sole Wonder, much less arm
> Thy looks, the Heav'n of mildness, with disdain,
> Displeased that I approach thee thus, and gaze
> Insatiate, I thus single, nor have fear'd
> Thy awful brow, more awful thus retir'd.
> Fairest resemblance of thy Maker fair,

> Thee all things living gaze on, all things shine
> By gift, and thy Celestial Beauty adore
> With ravishment beheld, there best beheld
> Where universally admir'd.

It is an all too human seduction. The practice of Poetry is morally conse-
quential, inevitably revealing something of the ethos of the poet.

There are very few living poets who are admired for their ethos. In
the network of gossip that comprises the constant underlying murmur
of the poetry business, when there is news, most of it is about who's been
fired for sexually harrassing students, who is ill, or who has died recently.
If the attention of the general public were as caught up with events in the
poetry world as it is with Hollywood, and if the monetary stakes were
higher than they are, there would be a monthly tabloid newspaper, PO-BIZ,
like *Variety* or the *National Enquirer*. There isn't. The art of poetry remains
comparatively pure, and this is a good thing. There is a measure of moral
and aesthetic shelter in privacy. Auden put it beautifully at the end of
"September 1, 1939":

> Defenceless under the night
> Our world in stupor lies;
> Yet, dotted everywhere,
> Ironic points of light
> Flash out wherever the Just
> Exchange their messages:
> May I, composed like them
> Of Eros and of dust,
> Beleaguered by the same
> Negation and despair,
> Show an affirming flame.

William Stafford said something similar in "Deerslayer's Campfire Talk":

> Wherever I go they quote people
> who talk too much, the ones who
> do not care, just so they take the center
> and call the plans.
> When I see these things, a part of my

mind goes quiet, and by a little turn
of my eyes I favor what helps, and ordinary
men, and that dim arch above us we seldom
regard, and—under us—the silent,
unnoted clasp of the rock.

The marginality of poetry, which has so often been scorned by critics like
Joseph Epstein, is a kind of strength: it will always keep American poetry
relatively pure.

American Male Poetry
of Sensibility

In WENDELL BERRY's famous essay "The Specialization of Poetry," he writes:

> One of the oldest doctrines of specialist-poets is that of the primacy of language and the primacy of poetry. They have virtually made a religion of their art, a religion based not on what they have in common with other people, but on what they *do* that sets them apart. For poets who believe this way, a poem is . . . a seeking of self in words, the making of a word-world in which the word-self may be at home. The poets go to their poems as other people have gone to the world or to God—for a sense of their own reality.

One result of this is the production, especially in our better-known poetry workshops, of a kind of narcissistic poetry that might be termed, to borrow the word often applied to poets of the late eighteenth century, like Thomas Gray, a poetry of *sensibility*.

Sensibility has a long lineage. The entry on "s." occupies a full page and a half of *The Princeton Encyclopaedia of Poetry and Poetics*. It begins:

> SENSIBILITY first became prominent as a literary term in the mid-18th c., with the meaning "susceptibility to tender feelings." It links the (possibly undesirable) quality of feeling sorry for oneself and conscious of one's own woes, with a morally praiseworthy quality—susceptibility to the sorrows of others—and an aesthetically praiseworthy quality, responsiveness to beauty.

The term immediately calls to mind such conspicuously sensitive types as Goethe's young Werther, Charles Baudelaire, Ernest Dowson, and, of course, Oscar Wilde. When it comes to poets, the term seems to be conventionally associated with men. It is almost equivalent to "sensitivity" but with this difference: it is *cultivated* sensitivity. According to Berry, it is the stock in trade of the contemporary specialist-poet, a figure who is, for Berry too, implicitly male:

> To how great an extent is modern poetry the record of highly refined sensibilities that could think or feel but not do? And must not this passiveness of the poetic sensibility *force* its withdrawal into the world of words where, for want of the sustenance of action, it becomes despondent and self-destructive?

One immediately thinks of the famous anecdote about Wilde, who, when asked what he had done today, replied that he spent the morning deciding to remove a comma from a line of his poetry. "And what did you do in the afternoon?" "I spent it deciding to put the comma back in." (The same story is told of Brahms; but instead of a comma the figure is a quarter note. Probably both stories are apocryphal: like the folkloric notion that the Eskimo has fifty words for snow, they are metaphorical shorthand for intense aesthetic activity.) But Berry is right, I think, when he says in the same essay, "The danger may not be so much in the over-cultivation of sensibility as in its *exclusive* cultivation."

University-based, male poetry of sensibility may be epitomized by the following poem. The poet recalls encountering his ex-lover in Paris. It is a prose poem, but I will reproduce here the "line breaks" of the paragraph.

> Another time I run into Zoe as she is coming out of a *parfumerie*.
> It's just past 6:00; the dark is falling. She is wearing a bright red
> *Chinois* scarf, and her hair is cut in a way I haven't seen before.
> We talk very briefly, but as we do the passersby BEHIND ME are
> reflected in turn in the huge store window that looms up
> brightly BEHIND HER. Which makes us seem leaning together
> as the world hurries past around us—like two people joined in

some inexorable way. Finally, in parting, I ask if she is happy—
to which she laughingly says, you will have to smell me to know
for sure.
She is walking away from me, well down the street, barely in
sight, before I can bring myself to turn and—avoiding any CON-
SPICUOUS GESTURES (like one of the faceless passers by)—walk off
in the other direction.

The poem reminds me of a scene from a Woody Allen movie. Its main
subject is the poet's sense of the beauty—the poignant decorum—of his
own emotional life. In its focus on the poet himself, it resembles much
of the poetry of the English Romantic movement, but its subject is not,
as in Wordsworth, the poet's imagination. Nor does it present the poet as
a heroic outsider. Instead, its subject is the poet's refined sensibility. Coy
and narcissistic, the poem functions like a glossy clothing advertisement
in *Vanity Fair*. The poet has been expelled from Eden, and, in the words of
the book jacket, his book (*The City of Women*) is "a sustained meditation on
the nature and origins of erotic love."

Probably the single best piece of writing about men's poetry that I
know of is an extended review-essay of Dave Smith's poetry, by Paul
Christensen in the fall/winter 1984 issue of *Parnassus*. The essay's title is
"Malignant Innocence," and Christensen's theorizing about men's poetry
is Jungian:

> The goal of the modern poem of reminiscence is to perform a miracu-
> lous ruse, outwitting nature and life—to put one's elder blood and
> mind into youth to witness, like Tiresias, all one's crises and miracles
> again, but with the wisdom one didn't have the first time. . . . Only in
> art, the fictive leap from life, can one pretend to return like a wise old
> ghost to the child again, just at the moment of epiphany.

Christensen then links the "poetry of reminiscence" with "a figure called
[by the Jungian psychologist James Hillman] the *puer eternus*" and with

the fictive persona Hillman calls the *paedogeron*, the young elder. The desire to be the knowing innocent, the infant sage in whom all polarities are resolved—the perfect, whole, united thing, the seamless mind and flesh, the knower and discoverer at once.

In the essay's most daring and far-reaching move, Christensen links "the poetry of reminiscence" with Symbolist poetry in general.

> Symbolist tradition on both sides of the Atlantic, beginning with Poe . . . is essentially a tradition of the *puer* myth . . . A common metaphor of the *puer* is the swan, that creature imprisoned in a pond, who is as white as the ethereal soul, and who sings when it departs this world of sorrows. . . . The swan as *puer*/poet is the flightless bird, who swims in a pool of its own reflection, trapped in its beautiful reveries. Dowson's rendering of Paul Verlaine's "Colloque Sentimental" gives us . . . the pond where the swan once sang its notes, where two enfeebled lovers recall their affair with much regret. . . . But shoals surround all such momentary epiphanies—every symbolist poem is ringed in sentimentality, hollow rhetoric, exhortation, the faked seance, the wooden ghost of youth, the shrill chest-beating and anxiety of the unrequited voice.
>
> Pity, self-pity in particular, is the integral function of symbolist writing; . . . All that remains of nature in the city is the image of woman.

That the poem I have chosen above as an example of the "poetry of sensibility" is a weak poem doesn't mean that poems that spring out of the puer myth are inherently weak. The puer myth is an archetype. Its structure informs the lives of all men, in whatever walk of life they have chosen. When they are writers, we get to view their inner lives more frankly and in greater detail than we do the lives of nonwriters.

To put the matter another way, all male poets use their art to display sensibility, in much the same way that the vivid red of the male cardinal or the spectacular open fan of the male peacock's tail exist in order to attract a mate and to mark territory: it's part of the job description. Whether they do so successfully, or wallow in the swan pond, will of course depend on talent; but talent is not enough. It will depend on something much harder to measure: character. To a significant extent, I think, the stature of a person's character may be measured by his or her interest and involvement in the world beyond the self.

An example of a poem that displays the structure of the puer myth, and also a finely attuned sensibility, yet which transcends the staleness of the swan pond, is Mark Jarman's "Ground Swell," a poem about adulthood and the passage to it:

> Is nothing real but when I was fifteen
> going on sixteen, like a corny song?
> I see myself so clearly then, and painfully—
> knees bleeding through my usher's uniform
> behind the candy counter in the theatre
> after a morning's surfing; paddling frantically
> to top the brisk outsiders coming to wreck me,
> trundle me gawkily along the beach floor's
> gravel and sand; my knees ached with salt.
> Is that all I have to write about?
> You write about the life that's vividest,
> and if that is your own, that is your subject,
> and if the years before and after sixteen
> are colorless as salt and taste like sand—
> return to those remembered chilly mornings,

And here, having made the necessary disclaimers, Jarman produces an epiphany:

> the light spreading like a great skin on the water,
> and the blue water scalloped with wind-ridges
> and—what was it exactly?—that slow waiting
> when, to invigorate yourself you peed
> inside your bathing suit and felt the warmth
> crawl all around your hips and thighs,
> and the first set rolled in and the water level
> rose in expectancy, and the sun struck
> the water surface like a brassy palm,
> flat and gonglike, and the wave face formed.

Yes. But that was a summer so removed
in time, so specially peculiar to my life,
why would I want to write about it again?

Jarman then begins to answer the question with a story. The story, like all achieved narration, pulls the storyteller out of himself, out of the nostalgic, potentially paralyzing reverie of the swan pond.

There was a day or two when, paddling out,
an older boy who had just graduated
and grown a great blond moustache, like a walrus,
skimmed past me like a smooth machine on the water,
and said my name. I was so much younger,
to be identified by one like him—
the easy deference of a kind of god
who also went to church where I did—made me
reconsider my worth. I had been noticed.
He soon was a small figure crossing waves,
the shawling crest surrounding him with spray,
whiter than gull feathers. He had said my name
without scorn, but just a bit surprised
to notice me among those trying the big waves
of the morning break. His name is carved now
on the black wall in Washington, the frozen wave
that grievers cross to find a name or names.

The poem ends:

Yes, I can write about a lot of things
besides that summer that I turned sixteen.
But that's my ground swell. I must start
where things began to happen and I knew it.

What is it, beyond Jarman's verbal talent, that makes "Ground Swell" so much more than a display of mere sensibility, like the Zoe poem? It is, I think, our sense that Jarman has actually done something in the world, has risked more than words about it: he has risked his body in it. He has not, as the Zoe poet seems to have, spent most of his time indoors mooning around like Goethe's young Werther. Reading the poems of *The City of*

THE PRACTICE

Women is like listening to a friend talking about his own psychoanalysis: the dullest and most self-indulgent subject in the world. In fact, both the poem (and the book) invite the reader into the position of a psychoanalyst.

Sheer verbal talent can, as Christensen suggests, go some way toward faking the semblance not only of personal character for a poet but a semblance of life lived. The Zoe poem attempts to create a word-self that is superior to the poet's "real" self and then substitute this word-self as a veneer to cover the absence of an authentic self. It dons the worldly looking costume of a life the poet may never have led. The power of Jarman's "Ground Swell," on the other hand, especially when contrasted to the Zoe poem, would suggest how difficult it is to fake authenticity.

In his book *Home: The History of an Idea*, Witold Rybczynski pointed out that Ralph Lauren's fashions and the interior-design packages that accompany them consciously imitate the movies. Thus in the suburbs in the late 1990s one can buy an authentic-looking World War II bomber pilot's jacket for just under two hundred dollars. Armed with the jacket, one can sit in a dimly lit bar smoking a Camel and look as world weary as Humphrey Bogart in *Casablanca*. In Banana Republic, one can buy interesting safari clothes with many practical-looking pockets, without ever having gone on a safari. In each case, the wearer lays claim not to firsthand experience but to vicarious experience. He deliberately advertises the fact that he has invested thousands of semester hours in the refinement of his own taste —in reading novels, watching television, attending movies. Part of him longs to be like Bogie, like Paul Newman, like Mel Gibson, to be a work of art himself, a star.

He can't be. He is only a university poet. Yet perhaps that is his job, to teach his own highly cultivated sensibility: to lay claim in public and in the classroom to his own wistful appreciation of real life and its suffering —his fear of it, his envy of it—to advertise and impart to his better students the aesthetic quality of his longing. He sees the presentation of personal character as a problem in rhetoric—"rhetoric" in the sense that politicians understand. To be believed and followed, one must seem to be believable, to be worthy. But to construct and maintain the image of public credibility is hard, and it is especially hard for poets, because, in addition to the usual demands of being a professor—to publish regularly in respectable places—poets are supposed to be, like mathematicians or violists, brilliant—brilliant on demand. This has resulted, in America, in the production of poetry on an industrial scale; but most of it, though alleged to be "brilliant," is not. Let us look at some of the evidence.

Character Weakness

Mauvaise Foi

THE IDEAL OF Authenticity in products, in personal behavior, and in art is, as Lionel Trilling once pointed out, highly problematical. But when I read, in the July 9, 1995, *New York Times Book Review*, the headline of Daphne Merkin's review of Michael Ryan's *Secret Life*—"The Curse of Eros: The autobiography of a poet who has struggled to overcome his sex addiction"— my curiosity was piqued. In the odd world of Po-Biz, in which gossip is the principal form of news, Ryan was famous for his promiscuity, which led to his dismissal from the Princeton University faculty in 1981 after he had affairs with female undergraduates. Ryan was famous also as an excellent "younger" American poet. His first collection, *Threats Instead of Trees*, won the most prestigious first-book award in the country, the Yale Series of Younger Poets Prize. His third book, *God Hunger*, won the Lenore Marshall/Nation Award for the most outstanding book of poems published in 1989. He had received a Whiting Writers Award and a Guggenheim Fellowship. He was also a brilliant critic, perhaps the best poet/critic of his generation. His essay "Poetry and Audience," which I heard him deliver at Warren Wilson College when we were both on the staff there and which later appeared in the *American Poetry Review*, was breathtaking in its thoroughness and clarity. He was ahead of his time.

In *Secret Life* Ryan showed himself to be, if not still ahead of his time, then on the leading edge of American creative writing as the genre now known as "creative nonfiction" became fashionable. Creative nonfiction is replacing the dramatic lyric as the preferred genre for intensely personal reminiscence, particularly when such reminiscence is "confessional"—

when it is potentially embarrassing to its author. Indeed, confessional poetry such as Sylvia Plath's, Robert Lowell's, and Richard Hugo's was almost inevitably twinned with prose autobiography of one sort or another. Plath's *The Bell Jar* was the prose twin of poems like "Lady Lazarus." Hugo's essays (collected in *The Real West Marginal Way*) were the prose twins of poems like "The Lady in Kicking Horse Reservoir." Robert Lowell's *Life Studies* consisted of both prose family reminiscences and dramatic lyrics. The implicit purpose of what I have called "prose twins" is this: in order to understand the poems more completely, the reader is encouraged to read the available autobiographical gloss.

There is ample precedent, then, for books like *Secret Life*, and the conventions of public confession extend well beyond literature. Indeed, if the popularity of such TV shows as the *Jerry Springer Show* and the *Jenny Jones Show* are any indication, literature is no longer the preferred medium for confession. The term *tabloid journalism* is, in 1999, a cliché. This trend is another mark of the decline of serious literature to a position in which, with the exception of a few novels, such as Robert Stone's *Dog Soldiers* or Margaret Atwood's *The Handmaid's Tale*, it belongs: in the margins.

Secret Life is, in places, absolutely gripping—especially in the beginning. In the first chapter, "Soul Sickness," Ryan describes the kind of "trance" he would "go into" as he singled out a girl who had "The Look—pouting, furious, damaged, sullen," when for him

> the social world was a thin, irritating haze covering the real world of sex where we should be together. . . . My primary loyalty was to sex. No human relationship took precedence over it. Not marriage, not friendship, and certainly not ethics. Achievements were meaningless unless converted into sexual rewards.

In this chapter, though, the book's stylistic flaws show up almost immediately. Describing fantasies about sex with "a friend's fifteen-year-old daughter," he says:

> That night while her parents were asleep, she would sneak down to my room in her nightie, and that's when we'd do it seventeen ways from Sunday, and continue doing it every chance we got. Her ecstasy

would be unbounded. She'd have so many titanic orgasms she'd think she was an earthquake.

Perhaps this narrative voice—the voice of Ryan's persona—is supposed to be taken as an instance of dramatic irony; but its jeering, macho boastfulness is, for this reader, not amusing. And it is confusing, too; because some of the best parts of the book, particularly Ryan's description of being seduced at the age of five by an adult man, are impeccably rendered. They are heartbreaking. This other voice—the sardonic, boastful voice—doesn't ring true. I think it may be an example of *mauvaise foi* in the sense Sartre develops in *Being and Nothingness*, where he argues that bourgeois romantic love is in bad faith, that a woman lets herself be deceived when she allows herself to sink into the swoon of love in order to get a husband. She is acting. Ryan's chest-beating gestures of public piety likewise have the feel of an act. When he describes his decision not to seduce the fifteen-year-old he lapses into dramatic self-pity.

> Outside, kids pestered their parents for Cokes and snacks. Everybody looked fat, ugly, and stupid, but nobody else was alone. I didn't want their lives and I didn't want mine either. There was no life I wanted. I had no one in Boston to go back to, no reason to be anywhere. My friends were out of town or picnicking with relatives. I never felt more lonely than this, but I was still not as lonely as I imagine a child molester is—the deepest loneliness inside the deepest shame, an unsurvivable loneliness.

Because of its self-pity, this passage leaves me unmoved. It is a naked plea to the reader, a plea for love.

The next chapter, "Secret Life," in which Ryan recalls being seduced by a neighbor, Bob Stoller, is the best-written chapter in the book . . . and no wonder. It describes, with trembling authenticity, the darkest initiation. Initiations—rites of passage—are the principal subject matter of dramatic lyric poetry. Ryan knows this: much of his own verse—poems like "The Crown of Frogs" in *God Hunger*—describes initiations.

> The stairway to the attic was narrow and steep and unfinished and smelled like a cedar chest. It was like the rabbit hole in *Alice in*

Wonderland, only climbing not falling through the passage to another world. Before long it would be exactly that. Knowing what would happen there, I would feel a new emotion as he followed me up the stairs, a blend of wonder and dread. Even this first time the passage seemed mysterious and secret. . . .

When I had all my clothes off—it was freezing—Bob Stoller suddenly pulled the curtain back. I felt terror—I'll never forget it—I was naked and he loomed over me. Standing straight up, I didn't reach his waist. He seemed twice as big now as before, and the light behind him made him into a dark hulk. It was so sudden.

Stoller persuaded the child to take a bath, and in the bath to play with his own penis.

When it was still stiff, he brought over a towel and said to stand up in the tub and he would dry me off. I did stand and he . . . began rubbing me with the towel all over and now it felt good and dreamy and warm not like when he touched me before in the dressing stall and he told me to put my arms around his neck and steady myself while he did it and I did, in a swoon, the classic gesture of surrender and embrace.

If at that moment I had been able to scream and run away, or evaporate into the steamy air, I believe my whole life would have been different. But I was already gone.

Two pages later Ryan describes, again with heartrending authenticity, the way routine life appeared to him afterward:

At home, of course nothing tangible had changed, which was at once reassuring and terrifying—reassuring because the furniture, my family, the noises, smells, and movement were familiar, negotiable, I could make my way through them and still be part of them but now only partially, only superficially; there was now a deeper reality than this one with boiled potatoes steaming on the table in a blue china bowl and the family gathering for dinner from their separate enterprises, this facade I'd never fully believe in again.

Ryan then delivers the core argument of this book:

the most insidious part of sexual abuse is in the creation of desire in the molested child, the way it forms a shape for desire that can never again be fulfilled, only compulsively substituted for and repeated, unless—if he's lucky and can find help—he ceases to identify with the molester.

This is plausible, yet how far should it be pressed? Indeed, it's merely the premise of much Freudian psychology, given additional spin by neo-Freudians like Jacques Lacan, whose hypothesis of the "mirror stage" advances the notion that because a child is learning language at the same time it is discovering that it is separate from its mother, the exercise of language is an inherently elegiac activity that aches with desire: words are inadequate substitutes for the original wholeness. The experience of molestation is not, then, the *only* source of what Ryan calls a "desire that can never again be fulfilled, only compulsively substituted for and repeated": so is the separation of every child from its mother.

The first two chapters establish a position: that the molestation formed the shape of Ryan's unappeasable desire, the sexual addiction that led to his being fired from Princeton in 1981. Provocative as this is, however, in the context of the remainder of the book it begins to look adventitious. Much of what follows records the trivia of a dreary, proletarian life, as Ryan's father was forced to move the family from one place to another, one job to another. In a tone of disillusionment, Ryan describes his child-hood girlfriends, his experiences playing Little League baseball, his minor initiations in high school, his time at Notre Dame, all in the kind of detail that one might spill out to a psychoanalyst. As I read Ryan's account, I was reminded of the famous comment by the actor Peter Lorre (who had stud-ied with Freud) that psychoanalysis was like "examining life through the asshole." Much of the prose is boring. And much of it is overwritten:

> His parents, unless they were comatose, must have heard him too. Heartbreak Hotel had a muffler designed to broadcast the music of its chromed, fuel-injected 409-horsepower engine to the frontiers of the civilized world. Plus Tommy was a virtuoso of the downshift. As he pulled in, it sounded like the driveway was being strafed.

or:

> Fifteen couples pressing and caressing as if to fuse their nervous systems, and feeling the pressure where their bodies connect travel from hairlines to toe tips. Fifteen beings made of thirty, shoulder to shoulder, radiating heat. There were enough pheromones in that basement to ripen a warehouse of green peaches.

I could quote such passages ad nauseam. The problem is that Ryan, when writing about the banalities of the fifties, is writing as though for a teenager; a teenager is the implied reader for the middle two-thirds of the book.

Ryan strikes an appropriate tone only when, as in the chapter about his seduction by Stoller, he veers away from trivia. In the strongest parts of the book the implied reader is a compassionate grown-up. In other well-done passages, Ryan confronts his father's drinking problem (the elder Ryan died of alcoholism at fifty-five, having suffered a third heart attack):

> He went to the doctor every other Tuesday and came home with blood pressure readings of 240 over 160 and up. Besides the eggs in the morning, he ate steaks and chops for both lunch and dinner. He smoked two packs of Pall Malls and drank about a fifth of whiskey every day. . . . He couldn't walk up two flights of stairs without catching his breath for a few minutes on the middle landing. It must be awful to live in a body like this, sick every morning, dragging until lunch when he'd have two or three Manhattans, enough to dull the edges and lighten the heaviness until five o'clock, when the serious drinking began.

As I have mentioned, the conventional dramatic lyric is a poem of memory, a poem that both describes remembered initiation experiences and, in its structure and language, reenacts them. It begins with a speaker in a condition of relative blindness. The story of such a poem is the story of how the poet's blinders were removed. At its best, the poem renders the process through which the poet transcended one version of himself and became a newer, "better" version. The motive behind such poems, as behind a prose autobiography like *Secret Life*, is the desire to clarify one's life, to know. Both a dramatic lyric and a prose autobiography begin half blind.

A good paradigm of this "revision" process in confessional lyric would be Richard Hugo's "The Lady in Kicking Horse Reservoir." The poem begins with Hugo gloating vengefully over the imagined drowning of a girlfriend who had dumped him:

> Not my hands but green across you now.
> Green tons hold you down, and ten bass curve
> teasing in your hair. Summer slime
> will pile deep on your breast. . . .

He recalls the past:

> We still love there in thundering foam
> and love. Whales fall in love with gulls
> and tide reclaims the Dolly skeletons
> gone with a blast of aching horns to China.

The poet recalls a dream in which a self-pitying boy is called to account:

> One boy slapped the other. Hard.
> The slapped boy talked until his dignity
> dissolved, screamed a single "stop"
> and went down sobbing in the company pond.
> I swam for him all night. . . .
> Morning then: cold music I had never heard.

The poet forgives the lover:

>   My hope is vague.
> The far blur of your bones in May
> may be nourished by the snow.
>
> The spillway's open and you spill out
> into weather, lover down the bright canal
> and mother . . .

The insight Hugo achieves at the end is that his fury at the woman who had dumped him goes back to his being abandoned by his mother. The poem embodies in miniature by a kind of self-psychoanalysis the process

of discovering this. By the end of the poem, the poet has been changed
—permanently.

Michael Ryan's *Secret Life* is preeminently a poet's book. All its most
powerful episodes describe initiation experiences. But I am not at all sure
if, by the end, Ryan has grown from the ordeals he has replayed. There is
something obligatory-sounding in the public resolution he makes in the
final pages:

> I got up and wrote this in my journal:
>
>> I am no longer Bob Stoller. Being him holds no appeal for me any-
>> more: he is a wriggling worm. . . . A benevolent, loving God has
>> replaced Bob Stoller. This is the gift, a surprising gift, better than
>> anything I could have asked for or imagined: myself. I can begin
>> to be my (God-given) self.

The conventional ending of twelve-step programs is religious. This passage has the rote sound of an obedient student trying too hard to pass a
test. He can talk the talk, but can he walk the walk?

More interesting and much more convincing is the dream Ryan
recounts near the end:

> I dreamed only once in my life about Bob Stoller—in August 1991
> . . . eight months after I wrote out my bottom-line behavior on a
> plane to California and almost a year after I found myself driving to
> upstate New York for the purpose of seducing my friend's fifteen-
> year-old daughter. I was working on this book, and trying to break
> the pattern of compulsive seductions one day at a time, to see exactly
> what was behind it and if I could begin to become a person who
> could be happy. . . .
> I dreamed I had somehow gotten in touch with Bob Stoller.

The mention of "this book" reflects Ryan's semiautomatic impulse to give
his narrative the self-reflexivity of a dramatic lyric. But the dream Ryan
recounts is a dilly, so complex and interesting that I must invite the reader
to look it up for him- or herself. The dream provides a fitting epiphany
for the ending of this haunting but seriously flawed book.

The flaws are not entirely Ryan's fault, though. Some lie in the genre of creative nonfiction itself, particularly at this historical moment (1999), when reportage, both in newspapers and on television, has acquired increasingly the aspect of "tabloid" journalism. Our country is inundated with hearings and trials involving American sexual mores: the confirmation hearings surrounding Clarence Thomas's alleged sexual harassment of Anita Hill, the O.J. Simpson trial, the impeachment of President Clinton, and, in the poetry world, the dismissal of some famous, tenured male full-professor poets for alleged "sexual harassment." But the reasons behind our "tabloid" culture and the sexual issues of *Secret Life*—issues I will now touch upon in the chapter "Sex and Poetry"—are grounded in American culture and its Puritan heritage.

Sex and Poetry

Poetry that attempts to describe in concrete detail sexual intercourse will usually disappoint and possibly offend. The reasons for this have to do with morality, epistemology, and (of course) artistry. All this was brought home to me when reading, in the twentieth anniversary issue of the *American Poetry Review*, a poem by Galway Kinnell entitled "The Night." The poem begins:

> Just as the paint leaps off the brush
> onto the clapboards that have gone fifty years unpainted
> and disappears into them almost with a slurp,
> so the words of these two who lie talking
> with mouths almost touching seem to pass
> from one mouth into the other without
> any sound except small lip-wetting smacks.
> Now the mouths touch and linger on each other,
> making little eating motions with suction squeaks.
> She licks a wet, slithery language on his chest,
> looks up, smiles, shines on him three actual words,
> resumes the liturgical licking: . . .

The opening figure of the dry wood drinking paint is beautiful. It could have been put to good use in a poem about sexual love, if such a poem were about a couple who had undergone a prolonged period of sexual deprivation or absence of human touch at all. Suddenly they have rediscovered the kind of knowledge that comes with sexual completion. In fact, the poem ends with a gesture in that direction. But before it makes its final gesture it indulges in more description and some coy, self-satisfied wit:

> He touches her where she glisses wet and shining
> as the lower lip of a baby tantalizing its gruel bowl
> with lengthening and shortening dangles of drool:

"The Night" is not a bad poem, it's a lazy poem. Its free verse is slack and garrulous. Its selection of details is indiscriminate. Much of it is like a description of food, a gourmet meal. It might have been a better poem if it had simply omitted the "gruel bowl," the "dangles of drool"; for the ending of the poem is splendid. The lines, which link "The Night" with the tradition of the aubade, beautifully render two lovers gradually awakening after a night of love:

> She wakes, but they do not get up yet, it is not
> easy to straighten out bodies that have been lying
> all night in the same curve, like paint brushes
> left all winter in a can of evaporated turpentine.
> They listen to the bony clangs of a church clock. Why only nine?
> When they have been living since the earth began.

The clangs of the church clock suggest that it might be Sunday morning (indeed, "The Night" might be construed as an implicit response to Wallace Stevens's "Sunday Morning"). The paintbrush motif that had begun the poem has been elegantly completed. But this ending has been compromised somewhat by the descriptions that precede it.

The "moral" problem of the poem is one of taste. The poem is both a boast and a sexual invitation to any women in the audience. In this respect, it recalls the poetic persona of the late James Dickey, who, before giving a poetry reading, reportedly would advertise his availability afterward. Dickey's poem, "Adultery," describes, shamelessly (but with utter accuracy) the emotional landscape of adultery:

> There is always some weeping
> Between us   and someone is always checking

A wrist watch by the bed to see how much
Longer we have left. Nothing can come
Of this   nothing can come

Of us: of me with my grim techniques
Or you who have sealed your womb
With a ring of convulsive rubber:

Although we come together,
Nothing will come of us. But we would not give
It up, for death is beaten

The poem's raison d'être is probably that of all realist art—to give the reader a shock of recognition and a vocabulary for his own experience; but the excuse which the poet gives—that the lovers do this in order to cheat death—is a lame one. The real reasons why people indulge in adultery are much more venal, the stuff of novels like *Madame Bovary*. Dickey's poem is soap opera, and the admission into his poem of the pronoun "I" turns it into a boast and calls the character of Dickey's persona into question. Is this somebody that we could admire?

Though Kinnell's "The Night" is in better taste than Dickey's "Adultery," it functions much as Freud theorized that jokes function in *Jokes and Their Relation to the Unconscious*, as a vehicle for sexual aggression. Like an exhibitionist, the persona is coyly "flashing," whispering to the audience, *I know and truly appreciate all these luscious sexual details. Just listen!* But like the Dickey poem, it is in bad faith, because such whispers normally comprise a *private* meditation. There is no reason to broadcast them in print or in a poetry reading before a live audience in such detail unless to advertise oneself to potential lovers; for there is not one of the pleasures which the poem celebrates that all, compatible, well-practiced lovers haven't enjoyed as often as they wished. Why can't the persona simply bask in his memory of pleasure privately, knowing he can go back for more whenever he wants to? Why must he make such a big deal out of it in *public*?

One reason may be historical. Those us who, like Kinnell and Dickey, came of age sexually before the sexual revolution of the seventies, before the pill, tended and still tend to make more out of frank sexual disclosure than subsequent generations have. Think, for example, of Ginsberg's great poem *Howl*, Grace Metalious's best-seller *Peyton Place* or, ten years later, Erica Jong's best-seller *Fear of Flying*. "The Night" is out of key with its time. It is naive because, despite Kinnell's age, it has an adolescent quality.

A second and related reason has to do with literary fashion. "The Night" commits resolutely the standard, almost obligatory error found in poetry in the deep-image tradition. Though the poem is realistic, the poetic persona speaks in an archetypal style, pious and solemn. Whitman had been able to poke fun at himself and to approach his reader almost like a stand-up comedian:

> Is this then a touch? quivering me to a new identity,
> Flames and ether making a rush for my veins,
> Treacherous tip of me reaching and crowding to help them,
> My flesh and blood playing out lightning, to strike what is hardly
>   different from myself,
> On all sides prurient provokers stiffening my limbs,
> Straining the udder of my heart for its withheld drop,
> Behaving licentious toward me . . .
> Unbuttoning my clothes and holding me by the bare waist,
> Immodestly sliding the fellow-senses away,
> They bribed me to swap off with a touch, and go and graze at the
>   edges of me,
> No consideration, no regard for my draining strength or my
>   anger,
> Fetching the rest of the herd around to enjoy them for awhile,
> Then all uniting to stand on a headland and worry me.
>
> The sentries desert every other part of me,
> They have left me helpless to a red marauder,
> They all come to the headland to witness and assist against me.

This is one of the funniest, most joyous passages of poetry that I know of. It's like a stand-up comedy act, but it's not dirty. Whitman is shame-less here, and that is the very point of the passage. He is attempting to give the audience permission to let go of bodily and sexual inhibition. We watch him undressing himself on stage before us. The passage gets wilder. Now that the sentries have deserted him, his own bodily senses are assaulting him:

> I am given up by traitors;
> I talk wildly . . . . I have lost my wits . . . . I and nobody else am
> the greatest traitor,
> I went myself first to the headland . . . . my own hands carried me
> there.
> You villain touch! what are you doing? . . . . my breath is tight in
> its throat;
> Unclench your floodgates! you are too much for me.
> Blind loving wrestling touch! Sheathed hooded sharptooth'd touch!
> Did it make you ache so leaving me?

It is Whitman's humor which renders the passage above so transcendent. His "shamelessness" has an almost religious quality: it is a form of humility. In the Dickey passage, on the other hand, though it is as shameless as the Whitman, it is shameless in a different way, and it is without humility

In the Kinnell passage, instead of awe we find what we would expect in America, awe transformed into doctrine: piety. But the Puritan piety of the fifties and sexual description have never gone together comfortably. Even in the supposedly liberated nineties, what Kinnell hopes sounds reverent actually sounds slightly prurient, because it is.

Indeed, perhaps because the poem has such a cinematographical quality, it places the reader somewhat in the position of a voyeur. Like one of the love scenes between Richard Gere and Debra Winger in the movie *An Officer and a Gentleman*, it presents a cinematographical close-up of the lovers:

> so the words of these two who lie talking
> with mouths almost touching seem to pass
> from one mouth into the other without
> any sound except small lip-wetting smacks.
> Now the mouths touch and linger on each other,
> making little eating motions and suction squeaks.
> She licks a wet, slithery language on his chest,
> looks up, smiles, shines on him three actual words,
> resumes the liturgical licking.

We end up staring wistfully, almost voyeuristically, at Kinnell's picture of the lovers, as we might at a scenic landscape or a spectacular touchdown on television.

Increasingly, in a media-saturated environment, we study pictures of the physical world instead of grappling with the thing itself. We find ourselves in the position of spectators rather than participants, and I think again of Stafford's "Evening News":

> In the yard I pray birds,
> wind, unscheduled grass,
> that they please help to make
> everything go deep again.

The most successful poems about sexual experience avoid the weaknesses of "The Night." They tend to be formalist and to observe, like the poems of Yeats and Roethke, a strict decorum. Indeed, for the very reasons implicit in Richard Wilbur's famous analogy of "form" as that which is necessary to confine the power of content like a genie inside its bottle, when writing poetry about sex, a rather stringent form would seem to be almost a requirement for artistic success. Without such confinement, the genie is apt to drip out in "lengthening and shortening dangles of drool," to "almost start snoring." A particularly pleasing example of "form" as a necessary bottle would be Marilyn Hacker's "Villanelle":

> Every day our bodies separate,
> exploded torn and dazed.
> Not understanding what we celebrate
>
> we grope through languages and hesitate
> and touch each other, speechless and amazed;
> and every day our bodies separate
>
> us farther from our planned, deliberate
> ironic lives. I am afraid, disphased,
> not understanding what we celebrate
>
> when our fused limbs and lips communicate
> the unlettered power we have raised.
> Every day our bodies' separate

routines are harder to perpetuate.
In wordless darkness we learn wordless praise,
not understanding what we celebrate;

wake to ourselves, exhausted, in the late
morning as the wind tears off the haze,
not understanding how we celebrate
our bodies. Every day we separate.

The iterative structure of the villanelle, like that of the sestina, is the ideal one for rendering an obsessional frame of mind. This poem's "feeling" is embodied in its very structure, and the impossibility of finding adequate words for the persona's emotion is admitted at the very outset: "Not understanding what we celebrate / we grope through languages and hesitate / and touch each other, speechless and amazed." The poem miraculously manages to have it both ways: it *does* find adequate words.

In the best poetry, such absolutes as sexual knowledge and knowledge about death are virtually always handled, like the killings and suicides in Greek tragedy, offstage. They have to be, because language—even the best poetry—is unequal to them and must content itself with pointing toward. Some kinds of absolute knowledge, for example the knowledge of physical pain, are impossible to approach in language at all, except with a groan or a scream. But such utterances are not art.

One final example of the virtues of indirection and of form in the handling of absolute knowledge would be Mark Cox's "The Blindness Desired." Although technically in free verse, the poem exhibits conspicuous form both in its extended metaphor and in the way its sentence structure winds up in order to deliver, with a kind of sigh, the climax of its last line—a moment beyond language:

Coming, we call it—
as if we've been summoned
and packed in one bag
and boarded the plane
to spend long hours aloft
with someplace to get to.
As if someone inside us,
perhaps the past itself,

is at last catching up,
turning the corner, panting,
as it has forever, just in time
to see another departure.
Oh, the past is always on foot
rags bound around its shoes,
but it catches a glimpse
now and then
of the future it sired,
and knows, from a distance, that child's
favorite color and special games.
The past *sees,* that's all.
And our arrivals, these heart-rending
announcements of ourselves,
what are they but the mutiny
of every other of our senses—
a moment
when the heart stops
and, its closed circuitry
like a door nudged open by a knee,
admits all of us.

In the end, whether or not one can write successfully about sexual knowledge, is more than a moral or an epistemological question. It is an artistic one, but it is "artistic" not just in terms of writing skill but in terms of character: the character of the artist. To construct and maintain an image with public credibility is hard, and it is especially hard for poets because poets are supposed to be, like mathematicians or concert violinists, brilliant—brilliant on demand. Not surprisingly, such a demand has created in America (where poetry is produced on an industrial scale) a poetry which, though alleged to be "brilliant," is all too often forced. Let us look at some of the evidence.

Rhetoricity

THE TERM rhetoric no longer, as when Aristotle wrote his treatise on it, refers to the art of oratory but refers more to "style." I still tend, however, to regard rhetoric as having something to do with persuasion. Who, when dealing with the public, doesn't desire credibility? In *Self and Sensibility in Contemporary Poetry* (1984), Charles Altieri employs a trick now fashionable among literary theorists. He coins a new noun by adding to a familiar noun the Latinate suffix -ity, thus creating an additional and, in my opinion, adventitious level of abstraction to the word. Thus, in contemporary literary theory, we find this chain of abstraction: *Narration* to *Narrative* to *Narrativity* (or *Narracity*). Altieri's neologism is *rhetoricity*. Altieri writes:

> the desire for sincerity or naturalness, for poetry as communication, seems continually in tension with the highly artificial means required to produce the desired effects at a level of intensity adequate for lyric poetry. The effort to create the image contradicts the image, and we find it hard not to become suspicious of the values claimed for the ethos of naturalness. If we prove so easy to move, or if we are so unwilling to ignore the artificial means required to produce the desired effects at a level of intensity adequate for lyric poetry, it becomes difficult to trust any of the emotions produced by claims for direct expression. . . . Unless one finds new models of emotion, there is no way to concentrate extended analyses of what I call "rhetoricity" into the compressed forms of attention the lyric demands.

This was published in 1984, about the poetry of the preceding decade, when the demographic facts of American culture skewed public opinion in the direction of youth—"Never trust anybody over thirty" was a fashionable directive—when "the ethos of naturalness" was overrated. Overrated: This is the agenda implicit in Altieri's warning. He is something of a prophet and social critic. Much of his book is troubled by the issues he raises here. He is bothered, justifiably (in the context of the period he is critiquing) by what is "claimed for the ethos of naturalness," an ethos too much taken for granted. He was right, and his term *rhetoricity* is a useful one.

Samuel Taylor Coleridge says something similar in his *Biographia Literaria*, where he discusses the function of "metre" in poetry:

> As far as metre acts in and for itself, it tends to increase the vivacity and susceptibility both of the general feelings and of the attention. This effect it produces by the continued excitement of surprize, and by the quick reciprocations of curiosity still gratified and still re-excited, which are too slight indeed to be at any one moment objects of distinct consciousness, yet become considerable in their aggregate influence. As a medicated atmosphere, or as wine during animated conversation, they act powerfully, though themselves unnoticed.

"Though themselves unnoticed": Both Altieri and Coleridge long for "sincerity or naturalness" but find it difficult, in Altieri's words, "to ignore the artificial means required to produce the desired effects." The extreme intellectuality and introspection that makes Coleridge's *Biographia* such a timeless work of criticism had their cost. Coleridge's greatest poem, "Dejection: An Ode," is about how hard it is to write poetry and to be a theorist at the same time. The poem is plagued by "viper thoughts, that coil around my mind":

> they rob me of my mirth;
> But oh! each visitation
> Suspends what Nature gave me at my birth,
> My shaping spirit of Imagination.
> For not to think of what I needs must feel,
> But to be still and patient, all I can;
> And haply by abstruse research to steal
> From my own nature all the natural man—

This was my sole resource, my only plan:
Till that which suits a part infects the whole,
And now is grown almost the habit of my soul.

What Altieri calls rhetoricity is a two-edged sword. All poetry exhibits rhetoricity in that it is the product of rhetorical calculation, but when is such rhetoricity an impediment to writing and when is it a virtue? Does the issue of quality boil down to one of naturalness versus artificiality? Alas, it is not that simple.

First, as the history of literary taste makes plain, such criteria as "naturalness" and "artificiality" are entirely normative—matters of fashion. For example, the poems in Wordsworth's *Lyrical Ballads,* written, as Wordsworth asserted in his preface, "in the language really used by men," sound artificial when compared to Frost's dramatic monologues in *North of Boston.* Compared to the standard English "poetic language" that preceded them, however—to Thomas Gray or Alexander Pope—they sound *more* "natural."

Second, Altieri's contrast between "naturalness" and "artificial means" in poetry proposes a false dichotomy. All art, be it poetry, painting, or music, is artificial. Art is, by definition, artificial. What is natural and what is artificial, then, is entirely a matter of fashion, and the dichotomy is rendered even more problematical by that fashion known as the new formalism. Most end-rhymed new-formalist poems are weak, for a variety of reasons, which I will take up in the next chapter. They are conspicuously harder to write than vers libre; their rhetoric tends to be theatrical, to hype their subject matter or else to be overly polite; their subject matter tends to be more genteel than that of vers libre, and they value upper-middle-class gentility without question.

Let us first look at rhetoricity in general, and then, in the next chapter, admire and criticize the "rhetoric" of certain famous end-rhymed poems.

Like all critical concepts, a concept such as "rhetoricity" is virtually without meaning unless applied to actual poems. In an issue of the *Missouri Review,* we find the following passage of poetry by a younger female poet:

What do I have left? Lot erased
even my name, *Simone, meaning one who hears,*

and I did—the pitiful cries of my lover,
        my sisters, my friends, united in the terrible music
        of fire. . . .

Here the word *terrible* is an example of rhetoricity at its weakest. The word is a placeholder, arbitrary. Almost any word with painful connotations would do: "the sickening music / of fire," "the frightening music / of fire," "the awful music / of fire," "the sinister music / of fire," "the hideous music / of fire," etc. It's as if, reading the poem aloud, the poet visibly winced, or a tear escaped one eye, or her breath caught on the edge of a sob, or she physically approached somebody in the audience, grasped the poor victim by the shoulders, glared into the victim's eyes and insisted: "The music of fire is . . . is *terrible!*" Because of its oratorical quality, *terrible* might be accepted by the audience of a poetry reading; but without the stage props of an audience and the living presence of the poet, it fails. The poet seems to be trying too hard.

Another example—a more famous one—of a terrible use of "terrible" would be in Robert Bly's "Come with Me," which begins, "Come with me into those things that have felt this despair for so long— / Those removed Chevrolet wheels that howl with a terrible loneliness." Robert Bly, following his first collection *Silence in the Snowy Fields,* has become an entirely public poet, and this line might succeed in a public reading. But read silently it asserts an emotional claim that it cannot validate. It sounds histrionic. Would the line, read either aloud or silently, be weaker or stronger if we substituted a different adjective? I myself think that it would be equal in quality, or perhaps even improved, with some other adjective: "a desolate loneliness," or "a horrible loneliness," or "a miserable loneliness," or "a tattered loneliness," or "a derelict loneliness" or . . . the choices are endless.

The unfortunate cliché that good writing should show, not tell, though often misapplied, has some force here. I can think of only one instance, in a modern English poem, where the word *terrible* is, as workshop parlance would have it, "earned": Yeats's "A terrible beauty is born." The only other poem I can think of where the word is sufficient is in French, by Jacques Prevert—his famous poem that, describing a desperately hungry man staring through a restaurant window at food, begins: "Il est terrible / le petit bruit de l'oeuf dur casse sur un comtoir d'etain" (It is terrible, the tiny tap of the cracking of the hard-boiled egg on a tin counter).

As the demonstration above might suggest, one way of identifying what I'll call "weak rhetoricity" is by substituting some other word for the offending word. To see how this might work, let's look at a different cliché. As is well known, the adjective *dark* and the noun *darkness* were fashionable clichés in the vocabulary of the so-called deep-image poetry of the late sixties and early seventies. *Dark* really meant "hidden" or "secret" or "mysterious." James Wright's poem "Eisenhower's Visit to Franco, 1959," not one of his better poems, deployed *dark* and *darkness* carelessly, as a cliché:

> The American hero must triumph over
> The forces of darkness.
> He has flown through the very light of heaven
> And come down in the slow dusk
> Of Spain.
>
> Franco stands in a shining circle of police.
> His arms open in welcome.
> He promises all dark things
> Will be hunted down.

The reader can judge for himself what, if anything, is lost by substituting *secret* or *hidden* for *dark*, beginning "The American hero must triumph over / The hidden forces." Not much.

Unless deployed with the utmost care in a poem, all adjectives will look decorative—adventitious. In a weak poem in accentual-syllabic prosody, they will look suspiciously like padding; for example, in these lines by Frederick Feirstein: "I watch a jet plane's earnest, gray goose flight / Between the roofs: from your apartment here?/ I pull a tin ring off a can of beer." Why are words "tin ring" there, is the goose "gray"? Who would ever think this or say this? In vers libre, adjectives will exist mainly to flesh out certain sonic expectations. For example, why is the word "slow" in front of "dusk" in the passage above? It is to contribute, like seasoning in a salad, to the "oh" and "ow" sounds in the passage. Like the word *dark*, various colors have enjoyed fashion, for example the color "gray" (made fashionable by Richard Hugo), "white," and, briefly, "sepia." If there isn't already, there ought to be a Ph.D. thesis on this subject.

Just as colors, in poetry, come into and fall out of fashion, so also do metaphoric formulas. In the sixties, probably because *like* had so inhabited the vernacular—"it's like heavy, man, a heavy trip"—it was one of the most ubiquitous formulas in poetry. It has long since been replaced by other formulas. At present, the formulas that comprise the vocabulary of the standard workshop poem are: "How," "The Way a," "As if," and "Adjective-noun of noun." The first three of these are often used as the springboard for what I think of as "the discursive metaphor." The inventor of this technique—a method of *inventio*—was, I believe, David St. John, in his poems "Slow Dance" and "Hush," though it may have been the late Larry Levis, who was David St. John's officemate at the Iowa Writers Workshop. St. John's "Hush" was reprinted in 1986, in *The Morrow Anthology of Younger American Poets*. It is dedicated "for my son." It begins:

> The way a tired Chippewa woman
> Who's lost a child gathers up black feathers,
> Black quills & leaves
> That she wraps & swaddles in a little bale, a shag
> Cocoon she carries with her & speaks to always
> As if it were the child,
> Until she knows the soul has grown fat and clever,
> That the child can find its own way at last;
> Well, I go everywhere

Picking the dust out of the dust, scraping the breezes
Up off the floor, & gather them into a doll
Of you, to touch at the nape of the neck, to slip
Under my shirt like a rag—the way
Another man's wallet rides above his heart. As you
Cry out, as if calling to a father you conjure
In the paling light, the voice rises, instead, in me.
Nothing stops it, the crying. . . .

From reading other St. John poems, we know that the son to whom the poem is dedicated was stillborn. Once we know that, then the "form" of this poem, its "discursive metaphor," is almost overwhelming: it is grief itself, the hopeless filling of a void with words.

When "the way" is applied in a poem without as compelling an occasion as St. John's, however, it tends toward the decorative, to be a means of generating text for the sake of text, a manner. Consider, for example, the following passage from the poem "Need Increasing Itself by Rounds," by an otherwise excellent poet:

The way Lorene and I went back
For blackberries, the same hill
But hotter, the way I said
Doesn't that haze down there look like snow,
The way she said no,
The way we left the good canes
To the bottom of the hill . . .

The poem's title "Need Increasing Itself by Rounds" has the look of an afterthought, by which the poet gave herself permission to use the formula "the way" indiscriminately. To appreciate how adventitiously the formula is applied, hear how the passage sounds without it.

Lorene and I went back for blackberries,
The same hill but hotter.
I said
Doesn't that haze down there
Look like snow?

> She said *no.*
> We left the good canes
> To the bottom of the hill.

Without the formula, the poem has voice and verve. The addition of the formula, by drowning out the sense of individual voice, lends the poem a solemn drone, an oracular tone that is at odds with its lighthearted subject matter. "The way" portends a metaphor without delivering one.

In contemporary poetry and for the reasons which Altieri adduces—to produce a mimesis of intensity—the greatest temptation to rhetoricity lies in the domain of adverbs and adverbial constructions, starting with that most gratuitous rhetorical gesture, the words *very* and *really:* "How much do I love you? I love you *very* much. I *really* love you! I love you *utterly!* I'll love you *forever!*" Repetition is endemic to verse, and formulas such as "over and over," "again and again," "on and on," "faster and faster," "higher and higher," "harder and harder," "slower and slower" afford the poet both an opportunity for effortless repetition and a concomitant surge of urgency. As the catalogs of Whitman suggest, one can mechanically assemble something strongly resembling a poem by making a list, each of whose elements repeats something in the previous line:

> And I stand at the lonely window
> And the light on the lawn is long.
> And behind me the class waits, puzzled,
> And wonders what I am doing . . .

For a real, not hypothetical example of rhetoricity, consider the following passage from Sharon Olds's "Language of the Brag," a poem about childbirth:

> my belly big with cowardice and safety,
> my stool black with iron pills,
> my huge breasts oozing mucus,
> my legs swelling and darkening, my hair

falling out, my inner sex
stabbed again and again with terrible pain like a knife.
I have lain down.

I have lain down and sweated and shaken
and passed blood and feces and water and
slowly alone in the center of a circle I have
passed the new person out.

How much rhetoricity this poem contains I leave the reader to judge. The formulas such as "again and again" are almost too easy to apply. I offer this parody:

Spring comes and soon it will be summer,
over and over, the same green imperative,
the way a drill sergeant orders the greenest
recruit to do push-ups,
first the daffodils, now the roses, over and
over, again and again, year
after year, the same dark forces,
and soon it is autumn, again
and again, the false, bright colors,
the falling leaves, . . .

It is alarming how easy it was for me to crank out the passage above—by formula. The ease of it not only confirms all of Altieri's suspicions. It explains the existence of that entity that Donald Hall so justly and sarcastically labeled a "McPoem." It explains how thoroughly and insidiously fashion—the rhetorical gestures that make up any period style—influence creative writing. It explains why even the best poets I know, at a certain stage in their careers, are apt, inadvertently, to parody themselves, to rehearse all the rhetorical gestures which, twenty years ago, they had discovered for themselves and personalized.

Now, because the pressure to produce another poem, another book, is so insistent, such a poet may have a tendency to reach out instinctively like an aging athlete for a move that once worked for him, to go through that move again simply to get into action. Maybe the feel of it, like the rhythmic surge an ice-skater remembers stepping out on that slippery ballroom floor of ice and pushing off, will place the skater back entirely in that lost world of moving ice and wind, when he or she was young and in love or trying to endure and find words for a grief that seemed almost too large for words, and discovered (almost miraculously, it now seems) the mechanical advantage of, instead of sobbing, saying:

> The way a tired Chippewa woman
> Who's lost a child gathers up black feathers

"The way a . . ." The poet pushes off again. The ankles are weak. The poet remembers Jonathan Swift's "A Discourse on the Mechanical Operation of the Spirit" in The Tale of a Tub, a satire in which Swift describes how the Protestant, nonconformist street preachers in his day (like our contemporary television evangelists such as Jimmy Swaggart) had learned how to "mechanically" whip themselves up into passionate speech. (Swift compared it implicitly to public masturbation.) The poet wonders: *Am I guilty of this?*

"It's the way a . . ."

The poet decides to put such thoughts aside for now. There's a poem coming. He remembers Keats's definition of "Negative Capability." He thinks that he is beginning to feel something. *Yes.* He can remember what it felt like to feel. Whether it will be a McPoem or not, he won't know for a while. How he will appear in the poem doesn't matter to him, yet. At least he is writing again. Therefore authentic.

He is a writer: a word-self.

The Public Nature of
End-Rhymed Poems

LET US GRANT, for a moment, that the persona of a poem is what I and others have called a word-self. What is the character of this word-self? That often seems to depend, in contemporary American poetry, upon the type of poem the persona is asserting. A number of stereotypes have developed.

One of these stereotypes associates poems in form—sonnets and end-rhymed poems—with what, in the eighties, was called the new formalism. Probably because the first new formalist to achieve prominence was an attorney named Brad Leithauser, and his first collection, *Hundreds of Fireflies*, concerned itself with matters conventionally associated with the wealthy, the new formalist poet stereotype was a wealthy male. In the main publishing organ of the movement, *The New Criterion*, Leithauser published an archly toned essay called "Metrical Illiteracy." Ever since then, new formalism has been, rightly or wrongly, associated with the wealthy, and the character of the persona of the formalist poem has been perceived to be, by some, adult, uptight, and politically conservative. The character of the free-verse poet has been perceived to be liberal, younger, and sometimes, like the late Allen Ginsberg, libidinous out of principle.

If there be any truth to these stereotypes, it is borne out more in their poems than in the lives of the poets. As I mentioned earlier, most of the poets who achieved their highest recognition writing in free verse started out as formalists. William Stafford's early poem "Bi-focal" is in end-rhymed trimeter. Many of James Wright's poems in *The Green Wall* are end-rhymed, accentual-syllabic poems, and the title poem of *Saint Judas* is a sonnet. The later poems of these men are in free verse, and the subject matter of these poems is much more intimate and vernacular than that of their earlier formal poems.

We have looked at the differences with respect to verbal surface and with respect to the types of figurative language each mode seems to favor —local (vers libre) versus global (formal)—but nobody, so far as I can discover, has adequately described why the two modes are so different and how intrinsic the difference is. It is grounded in the respective methods of *inventio* favored by practitioners of vers libre, on the one hand, and practitioners of accentual-syllabic prosody, on the other. The methods are so incommensurable as to be mutually exclusive. I have worked in both modes, and I have some tentative ideas about why.

Free verse is arrived at primarily by a process of free association. A sonnet or an end-rhymed dramatic lyric is arrived at with more conscious calculation, with a theme already in view. Free verse tends toward subjectivity. End-rhymed poems in traditional forms tend to be less subjective than free verse, and this fact is reflected in their language. The contemporary dramatic lyric in free verse tends to contain secular metaphors with private associations. End-rhymed poems in an accentual-syllabic prosody tend to deploy public language and to take their metaphors from Freud, from religion, or from some other public form of discourse, such as famous literature or philosophy, as in Richard Wilbur's early and famous poem "Mind." The polarity is a familiar one, the romantic versus the classical—Wordsworth versus Pope.

Just how intrinsic the difference is, how fully the decorum of end-rhyme governs the subject matter, indeed, the very vision of a poem (its implicit ideology) can be best appreciated if examined in the context of literary history. There are substantial reasons why practitioners of free verse and rhyming poetry will tend to distrust each other: Artistic temperament and artistic ideology reflect one another with respect not only to artistic intention—why poems are made—but with respect to how they are made.

Perhaps the most famous formulation of the aesthetic of end-rhymed, accentual-syllabic poetry is Alexander Pope's *Essay on Criticism*, with its smug, neoclassical certainties:

> True Wit is Nature to advantage dressed,
> What oft was thought, but ne'er so well expressed;
> Something whose truth convinced at sight we find,
> That gives us back the image of our mind.
> . . . . true Expression, like the unchanging Sun,
> Clears and improves whate're it shines upon,
> It gilds all objects, but it alters none. . . .
> But most by Numbers judge a Poet's song;
> And smooth or rough, with them is right or wrong; . . .
> True ease in writing comes from art, not chance,
> As those move easiest who have learned to dance.
> 'Tis not enough no harshness gives offence.
> The sound must seem an Echo to the sense.

Who would not agree with Pope's formulation of "True Wit" as "Something whose Truth convinced at sight we find"; but who would not, at the end of this millennium, object to his smug, pedantic tone. Pope was writing for an audience that shared his worldview. The situation facing the contemporary poet is different. This difference was expressed well by W. H. Auden in his essay "The Poet and the City," in *The Dyer's Hand*:

> There are four aspects of our present *Weltanschuung* which have made an artistic vocation more difficult than it used to be.
> 1) *The loss of belief in the eternity of the physical universe. . . .*
> 2) *The loss of belief in the significance and reality of sensory phenomena. . . .*
> 3) *The loss of belief in a norm of human nature which will always require the same kind of man-fabricated world to be at home in. . . .* ["Man is the measure of all things"]
> 4. *The disappearance of the Public Realm as the sphere of revelatory personal deeds.*
> . . .

> The growth in size of societies and the development of mass media of communication have created a social phenomenon which was unknown to the ancient world, that peculiar kind of crowd which Kierkegaard calls the Public. . . . To join the public, it is not necessary for a man to go to some particular spot; he can sit at home; open a newspaper or turn on his TV set.
>
> A man has his distinctive personal scent which his wife, his children and his dog can recognize. A crowd has a generalized stink. The public is odorless.

Auden had always striven to be a public poet, wishing to believe—against the very evidence which he himself so accurately details in the passage above—that "the Public Realm" *could* be "the sphere of revelatory personal deeds," that one could, scientifically, employing the language of Freud and Marx, make a valid civic art. It was Auden who would proclaim that the great Broadway musicals of the 1950s were the equivalent to Greek tragedy. This is why his signal poems, such as "September 1, 1939," employed end-rhyme. Rhyme was part of his program. But the story of how that poem was composed describes an alienated man, for whom crowds and the public were only hypothetical—a sentimental ideal. The poem begins:

> I sit in one of the dives
> Of Fifty-Second Street
> Uncertain and afraid
> As the clever hopes expire
> Of a low dishonest decade:

The poet Anthony Hecht, in his book about Auden, *The Hidden Law*, writes that Auden's phrasing "one of the dives" is a way of indicating that "His bar is a humble one. . . . In *Memoirs of a Bastard Angel* Harold Norse reports:

> At the end of August [1939], when Wystan and Chester returned [from a trip to California], Chester and I spent our first night at a notorious gay bar called the Dizzy Club on West Fifty-second Street, three blocks from my room. The dive was the sex-addict's quick fix, packed to the rafters with college boys and working-class youths under twenty-five. From street level you stepped into a writhing mass of tight boys in tighter pants. . . . Having decided that he must see it, we

told Wystan, who loved sleazy dives, about the Dizzy Club. The next night, September 1, without our knowledge he went alone. . . . He didn't go to pick up a boy; however, aware of the age difference and quite shy, he would have selected one of the two unused corner tables at the rear of the bar, which was usually deserted except for those too drunk to stand, from which he could observe boys kissing and groping under the bright lights, packed like sardines pickled in alcohol. There he would begin to write the most famous poem of the decade."

At this point, the reader is perhaps ready to raise all kinds of objections to my apparent oversimplication: What about Emily Dickinson's poems? Aren't they subjective? What about the poems in W. D. Snodgrass's *Heart's Needle*? They aren't public! But they are, precisely in the terms described by Auden above. They pretend that "the Public Realm" is "the sphere of revelatory personal deeds." Their "public" quality is reinforced by their end-rhyming.

For an example of the process of *inventio* by a contemporary poet working in vers libre to contrast against the Auden, we might consider William Stafford's short essay "A Way of Writing," published in *Field* in 1970. Stafford writes:

A writer is not so much someone who has something to say as he is someone who has found a process that will bring about new things he would not have thought of if he had not started to say them. . . . It is like fishing. But I do not wait very long, for there is always a nibble —and this is where receptivity comes in. To get started I will accept anything that occurs to me. . . . If I let the process go on, things will occur to me that were not at all in my mind when I started. These things, odd or trivial as they may be, are somehow connected. And if I let them string out, surprising things will happen. . . . At times, without my insisting on it, my writings become coherent; the successive elements that occur to me are clearly related. They lead by themselves to new connections. . . . But I do not insist on any of that; for I know that back of my activity there will be the coherence of my self, and that indulgence of my impulses will bring recurrent patterns and meanings again.

There follows a nearly illegible handwritten draft of Stafford's notebook dated "15 December 1969," and then the following typed draft of a poem, entitled "Shadows":

> Out in places like Wyoming some of the shadows
> are cut out and pasted on fossils.
> There are mountains that erode when
> clouds drag across them. You can hear the tick
> of the light breaking edges off white stones.
>
> At a fountain on Main Street I saw
> our shadow. It did not drink but
> waited on cement and water while I drank.
> There were two people and but one shadow.
> I looked so hard outward that a bird
> flying past made a shadow on the sky.
>
> There is a place in the air where our house
> used to be.
>
> Once I crawled through grassblades to hear
> the sounds of their shadows. One of the shadows
> moved, and it was the earth where a mole
> was passing. I could hear little
> paws in the dirt, and fur brush along
> the tunnel, and even, somehow, the mole shadow.
>
> In churches these hearts pump sermons
> from wells full of shadows.
> > In my prayers I let yesterday begin
> > and then go behind this hour now.

The final version is almost exactly like this one, except that the third stanza reads, "There is a place in the air where / our old house used to be," and the last stanza reverses the order of the sentences, ending:

> In my prayers, I let yesterday begin
> and then go behind this hour now,

in churches where hearts pump sermons
from wells full of shadows.

The poem reminds us, in its fossil imagery, of that country's ambient geological history. Stafford captures a moment of loneliness and poignant déjà vu and distance—over a thousand miles between this scene in the mountains and the Kansas Stafford remembers—distance in the midst of sunlight. The poem's fleeting vision is almost entirely private—public only in terms of light and landscape.

To appreciate the difference between a good free-verse dramatic lyric like Stafford's and a good poem with end-rhyme, let's compare the Stafford poem to a section of W. D. Snodgrass's *Heart's Needle*:

> Late April and you are three; today
>   We dug your garden in the yard.
> To curb the damage of your play,
> Strange dogs at night and the moles tunnelling,
>   Four slender sticks of lath stand guard
>   Uplifting their thin string.
>
> So you were the first to tramp it down.
>   And after the earth was sifted close
> You brought your watering can to drown
> All earth *and* us. But these mixed seeds are pressed
>   With light loam in their steadfast rows.
>   Child, we've done our best.
>
> Someone will have to weed and spread
>   The young sprouts, sprinkle them in the hour
> When shadow falls across your bed.
> You should try to look at them every day
>   Because when they come to full flower
>   I will be off away.

The rhetorical feel of this passage is, like all of *Heart's Needle*, oratorical. This oratorical feel is not because the poem is addressed to a "you." There are plenty of poems addressed to a "you" that are intensely quiet, whispered or merely thought. But this poem's gestures are public. The three-year-old daughter is a stage prop, and the poet is booming his poem to an audience beyond her. His sentiments, trembling as they are with painful emotion, verge on the corny. They are conventionalized.

We can now begin to appreciate how thoroughly the convention of end-rhyme governs the decorum of a dramatic lyric. Even the most apparently intimate lyric, for example W. H. Auden's "Lullaby" ("Lay your sleeping head, my love") is oratorical, and its dissonances so often remarked on stem from its public character. In *The Hidden Law*, Hecht writes:

> Within the wide spectrum of love that this book and the previous one envisage, including love as mysteriously curative of both individual and social ills, the love described here [homosexual] is touching, vulnerable, and decently screened as regards gender. This may have been a sly and protective device, but it could just as easily be a trick Auden had learned very early from the popular song writers. . . . The Broadway musical writers he most admired had learned a simple economic fact: though in the context of one of their shows the dramatic realities might demand that a particular song be sung by a man to a woman or vice versa, much could be written so as to be sexually indiscriminate, and thus sung by either male or female vocalists for broadcast or recording purposes.

There is a sense in which most of Auden's poems, like Yeats's, are implicitly conceived of as theater pieces. In terms of Northrop Frye's "anatomy," their "radical of presentation" is what Frye termed *epos*. End-rhyming poems almost invariably use conventional imagery to project conventional sentiments, and it is in this respect that they constitute a public poetry: its sentiments are necessarily sanitized. To appreciate this, let us compare the Stafford poem to the following poem by Dana Gioia:

Summer Storm

We stood on the rented patio
While the party went on inside.
You knew the groom from college.
I was friend of the bride.

We hugged the brownstone wall behind us
To keep our dress clothes dry

And watched the sudden summer storm
Floodlit against the sky.

The rain was like a waterfall
Of brilliant beaded light,
Cool and silent as the stars
The storm hid from the night.

To my surprise, you took my arm—
A gesture you didn't explain—
And we spoke in whispers, as if we two
Might imitate the rain.

Then suddenly the storm receded
As swiftly as it came.
The doors behind us opened up.
The hostess called your name.

I watched you merge into the group,
Aloof and yet polite.
We didn't speak another word
Except to say goodnight.

Why does that evening's memory,
Return with this night's storm—
A party twenty years ago,
Its disappointments warm?

There are so many *might have beens*,
What ifs that won't stay buried,
Other cities, other jobs,
Strangers we might have married.

And memory insists on pining
For places it never went,
As if life would be happier
Just by being different.

This poem has some good touches: "Floodlit against the sky" is an accurately noticed detail, as is the image of "brilliant, beaded light." The metrical substitution in the last line is effective. But the poem's strict

emotional decorum is oppressive. The character of the persona is that of an uptight adult. It is corny, reminiscent of Auden's parody of popular music:

> You were a great Cunarder, I
> Was only a fishing smack,
> Once you passed across my bow
> And of course you did not look back.
> It was only a single moment, yet
> I watch the sea and sigh
> Because my heart can never forget
> The day you passed me by.

But Auden, in his Marxist phase, was satirizing bourgeois love. Gioia is not. Just how constricting Gioia's decorum is may be appreciated if we compare it to another poem by Stafford, "Behind the Falls":

> First the falls, then the cave:
> then sheets of sound around us fell
> while earth fled inward, where we went.
> We traced it back, cigarette lighter high—
> lost the roof, then the wall,
> found abruptly in that space
> only the flame and ourselves,
> and heard the curtain like the earth
> go down, so still it made the lighter
> dim that led us on under the hill.
>
> We stopped, afraid—lost
> if ever that flame went out—
> and surfaced in each other's eyes,
> two real people suddenly
> more immediate in the dark
> than in the sun we'd ever be.
> When men and women meet that way
> the curtain of the earth descends, and they
> find out how faint the light has been, how far
> mere honesty or justice is from all they need.

I assume that this poem doesn't need explication. Just how crafty it is may be appreciated if we consider the meaning of the word *immediate*, with its etymological connotation of "unmediated." "Behind the Falls" is not strictly end-rhymed, though, like all achieved poems, it evinces form. It could never be mistaken for prose. I think that an attempt at strict end-rhyme might well have destroyed it. As for the character of the persona: he is obviously a moral man; but he is open to surprise, and he is ruthlessly honest. The differences between the two poems seem to me to bear out some of the stereotypes of the poet-persona.

I know a good deal of poetry by heart, and most of it is end-rhymed. I have written a few poems with end-rhyme myself, and I am positive that it is harder to write poetry with end-rhyme than in vers libre. When it is done well, I'm left speechless with admiration: at Richard Wilbur's translation of Moliere's *Tartuffe*; at his translation of Apollinaire's "Mirabeau Bridge"; at William H. Crosby's translation of Charles Baudelaire's *Les Fleurs du Mal*, published with BOA Editions in 1996, a translation rather better than Richard Howard's: Crosby was able to preserve the end-rhymes.

The trade-offs between end-rhyming formalist poetry and vers libre are equal: high finish and memorability versus wider subject matter. Probably the best younger formalist writing today is R. S. Gwynn, and I leave the reader with this dazzling flourish, the final section of Gwynn's "Body Bags," a sequence of three sonnets, each sonnet remembering a boy that Gwynn knew who was killed in the Vietnam War:

iii.

> Jay Swinney did a great Roy Orbison
> Impersonation once at Lyn-rock Park,
> Lip-synching to "It's Over" in his dark
> Glasses beside the jukebox. He was one
> Who'd want no better for an epitaph
> Than he was good with girls and charmed them by
> Opening his billfold to a photograph:
> Big Brother. The Marine. Who didn't die.

He comes to mind, years from that summer night,
In class for no good reason while I talk
About Thoreau's remark that one injustice
Makes prisoners of us all. The piece of chalk
Splinters and flakes in fragments as I write,
To settle in the tray where all the dust is.

The quality of this poem will speak for itself. It's a public poem, against war, not just Vietnam but all war. The remark of Thoreau is similar in sentiment to Carolyn Forche's cry in her poem about the war in El Salvador, that we are all "exactly like netted fish," or Auden's in "September 1, 1939": "And helpless governors wake / To resume their compulsory game." The final ironic statement of "Body Bags" is that "injustice" invariably ends up "where the dust is"—relegated to the past, as if it were only History (as if History were only the past).

Yet the poem, for all its ironic brilliance, remains curiously impersonal, especially if compared to a poem like Stafford's "Evening News." Its *formal* brilliance seems to work against the kind of emotional intimacy we find in the best free-verse poetry. What does the author/persona *feel*? What is his character like? Do we trust him? In part 2 of this book, "Personae," we will take up this question. First, however, let us return to my book's main premise regarding form—its apology for free verse and its argument that the few people who oppose it do so for ideological reasons.

The Old Formalism

ONE OF THE biggest deceptions that muddies the contemporary American poetic milieu is something called the New Formalism. In what sense is the term *New Formalism* a deception? In nearly every sense.

Let's begin with the word *new*. Formalism has never been new. Such poets as Judith Moffett, Marilyn Hacker, Fred Chappell, Richard Moore, Sydney Lea, Lewis Turco, and R. S. Gwynn, to name but a few, have been working in forms for years. Indeed, except for Richard Wilbur and James Merrill, most of the American poets who in 1957 were featured in *New Poets of England and America* and demonstrated in that anthology their mastery of the forms later chose to work, with greater success, in free verse. To tack the word *New* (with a capital N) to the word *Formalism* is simply an advertising stunt—a rather tired stunt, I might add.

A more serious deception is perpetrated by the so-called New Formalists' identification of formalism with meter. "No verse is free for the man who wants to do a good job," Eliot wrote in his essay "The Music of Poetry," and he was right. In this chapter, I would like to argue two main ideas. The first is a paradox. Although the decorum of good free-verse composition differs from that of accentual-syllabic verse, good "free" verse is simply a medley of traditional prosodies. Secondly, the two possibilities for decorum can constructively overlap.

The most fundamental convention of verse has always been that it must maintain a conspicuous verbal surface. When accentual-syllabic prosody was the prevailing form of this convention—its normal form—poets could automatically fulfill the requirement. Meter, by foregrounding each discrete syllable within the context of the "foot," enabled a poet to draw attention to the verbal surface of a poem almost automatically, without resorting to conspicuous and forced figurative language. Reading Yeats, for example, we savor the sonic texture of his verses in much the same way that in a good, representational oil painting, if we admire it up close, syllable by syllable, as it were, we discover details in the disposition of the paint that we would never have expected—bits of alizarin crimson embedded in green grass, translucent strokes of blue in the flesh tone of a cheek—and these details have little to do with the painting's referential "content."

> Now shall I make my soul,
> Compelling it to study
> In a learned school
> Till the wreck of body,
> Slow decay of blood,
> Testy delirium
> Or dull decrepitude,
> Or what worse evil come—
> The death of friends, or death
> Of every brilliant eye
> That made a catch in the breath—
> Seem but the clouds of the sky
> When the horizon fades,
> Or a bird's sleepy cry
> Among the deepening shades.

The best poetry in an accentual-syllabic prosody happens at the level of the syllable. Each syllable is brought up into relief, bulges slightly like a discrete bead of paint. The sound of the Yeats passage is so much better than its sense that without that sound we might not pay particular attention to its sense. Its sense is conventional, without surprise. Paraphrased, it might read: "As I enter the twilight of life and my body breaks down, I am going, through the study of philosophy, to learn how to view myself and indeed the entire human condition *sub specie aeternitatis*."

In contemporary free verse, on the other hand, without the assurance of the metrical foot to call attention to the verbal surface of a poem, poets will, instinctively almost, turn to semantic means: stocking lines with conspicuous metaphors and similes, as if to compensate in the domain of "sense" for what they have had to give up in the domain of sound— as if, without such a surface, they would worry whether or not they were writing "poetry" at all. The Yeats passage above relies on an extended metaphor. In contemporary American "free" verse, on the other hand, we are apt to find a nervous, flailing assertion of figurative language. A good example might be the poem "Mind," by Jorie Graham:

> The slow overture of rain
> each drop breaking
> without breaking into
> the next, describes
> the unrelenting, syncopated
> mind. Not unlike
> the hummingbirds
> imagining their wings
> to be their heart, and swallows
> believing the horizon
> to be a line they lift
> and drop.

The difference in sense between free verse and end-rhymed accentual-syllabic verse, with its less assertive approach to figuration, might best be epitomized by a comparison between Graham's "Mind" and Richard Wilbur's early poem "Mind":

> Mind in its purest play is like some bat
> That beats about in caverns all alone,
> Contriving by a kind of senseless wit
> Not to conclude against a wall of stone.

It has no need to falter or explore;
Darkly it knows what obstacles are there,
And so may weave and flitter, dip and soar
In perfect courses through the blackest air.

And has this simile a like perfection?
The mind is like a bat. Precisely. Save
That in the very happiest intellection
a graceful error may correct the cave.

In postmodern poetry in accentual-syllabic verse, metaphors and similes will tend not, as in Graham's "Mind," to be deployed primarily for display. Like Yeats's sunset metaphor, or Wilbur's Platonic metaphor of the cave, they will be conventional ones, extended to make an argument, often a moral one.

The late-modernist mode employed by Wilbur alluded deliberately to the metaphysical poetry of John Donne; but, like the poetry of Eliot (who had rediscovered Donne and used Donne's poetry for his own purposes—to avoid emotional autobiography), it manifests a studied impersonality. It is curious that Jorie Graham's "Mind" is just as impersonal as Eliot, even though it is in free verse. Graham is one of the comparatively few contemporary poets whose verse, though it utilizes free association as a method of *inventio*, is not conspicuously subjective and emotional. It lacks a sense of personal voice. But it does manifest one characteristic of vers libre. Whereas the prosody of most end-rhymed, accentual syllabic verse is homogeneous, the prosody of Graham's "Mind" is, as I have already suggested, heterogeneous—a medley of traditional prosodies.

In the domain of both sound and sense, then, we note the following tendency. In accentual-syllabic poetry, the effects manifested both by prosody and metaphor tend to be global. In free verse, on the other hand, such effects tend to be local. To test this possibility, let us look at an example of good free verse, the following passage from "A Fugue," by Ellen Bryant Voigt:

The body, a resonant bowl:
the irreducible gist of wood,
that memorized the turns

of increase and relinquishing:
the held silence
where formal music will be quarried
by the cry of the strings,
the cry of the mind,
under the rosined bow.

In this passage, each of the first two lines coincides with a discrete metaphor. Free verse turns out to be the ideal prosodic vehicle for displaying to maximum advantage—for cherishing—individual units of figurative language, in much the same way that in an accentual-syllabic prosody *syllables* are fashioned to frame discrete sounds. Though its prosody is vers libre, however, the medley of traditional prosodies manifested in the passage above is distinct enough that the verse could never be mistaken for prose—as mere noise.

In his important but incompletely argued book *Free Verse*, the poet/critic Charles O. Hartman defined free verse as any "non-numerical prosody," by which he meant any verse in which neither syllables nor feet is counted. But just as counting is essential to music, counting is essential to poetry if that poetry is going to retain any of the properties of music. When trying to identify the traditional echoes of free verse prosody, I have found that a particularly efficient way is first to analyze free-verse lines as if they *were* ordered according to some numerical prosody—to try to scan them—then to arrange the same passage with line breaks that alter the relation between syntactical units and line units and observe how traditional prosodies which had not been immediately obvious but which had contributed subliminally to the medley are brought into franker relief.

1. The body, a resonant bowl:
2. the irreducible gist of wood,
3. that memorized the turns
4. of increase and relinquishing:

5. the held silence
6. where formal music will be quarried
7. by the cry of the strings,
8. the cry of the mind,
9. under the rosined bow.

Most of the lines seem to be in accentuals, with three stresses. Lines 5, 7, and 8, though, contain only two stresses. If we stress the word *by* in line 7 (for it follows an unstressed syllable and a line-ending pause), then line 7 is in trimeter. There is further inducement for us to interpolate trimeter in line 7, because the first several lines of this poem—lines which conventionally set our initial expectations about a poem's prosody —faithfully conform to syntactic units. They are *unequivocally* trimeter. They enable us later, in line 7, to hear in counterpoint both possibilities: dimeter and trimeter. We discover this kind of accentual counterpoint in other lines as well—in line 6, for example, where, if "will" is stressed we hear tetrameter; if it is not we hear trimeter. But the poem returns to its initially announced norm in the end, closing with three stresses which, because "resonant bowl" and "rosined bow" alliterate with each other so emphatically, they virtually rhyme. This "rhyme" gives the passage a pleasing (though hardly insistent) sense of symmetry, of closure. Accentuals then, in trimeter, make up what we might regard as the poem's foregrounded, or "primary," prosody. If it contains any other "secondary" prosodies, these are in the background. Are there others? Suppose we break the lines as follows:

1. The body, a resonant bowl: the irreducible
2. gist of wood, that memorized
3. the turns of increase and relinquishing:
4. the held silence where formal music
5. will be quarried by the cry of the strings,
6. the cry of the mind under the rosined bow.

Granted, the first two line breaks in this version are a bit forced; but the remaining four lines are plausible. These lines introduce the secondary prosody, which the poem contains in its alternate set of syntactical units.

This secondary prosody is, roughly speaking, that of blank verse, introduced in line 3. Line 4, though it contains only nine syllables, contains a tenth "ghost" syllable in the caesura following "silence." Line 5 contains exactly ten syllables. Line 6 has eleven syllables, but its fourth word, the lowly article "the," retains such a weak presence in the audial context of the line as a whole that it is easy for us to hear the old pentameter trying to assert its existence under the verbal surface—"the cry of the mind under the rosined bow"—a presence which is further strengthened by the fact that if we put lines 7 and 8 of the original together, we get another nearly decasyllabic unit: "by the cry of the strings, the cry of the mind," a unit which the ear, trained by line 3 in the revision ("the turns of increase and relinquishing"), can "hear" as decasyllabic by suppressing any of the three instances of "the." Was *all* this intentional? I doubt it. Such a beautiful, natural prosodic medley is more probably the result of a poet's ear, if her ear is good and well schooled in the tradition. A good, trained ear is, I believe, apt to hear an echo of iambic pentameter in *any* foregrounded decasyllabic unit.

This fact would suggest that the most fundamental rhythmical unit in verse is *not* the line but the syntactical unit. If so, then line length and line breaks, apart from their capacity to allude to a numerical prosody, would seem to be irrelevant to the effect of verses. The revision of the Voigt passage foregrounding the pentameter would therefore be equal in quality to the original passage. Is it? Obviously not. But why? It's a matter of decorum: propriety. The short, mainly trimeter lines of the original lend it a grave, stately pacing, a quality of rapt attention: adagio. The longer lines of the revision lose the sense of simplicity and reverence that lent the original such charm, such quiet seriousness. As our eyes travel from the left-hand margin all the way out to each line ending, they skim over the material. The language does not keep the same pace as the poet's attention. We watch it, before our eyes, about to slip into what Pound so accurately called "perdamnable rhetoric."

In the hands of a poet as skillful as Voigt, free verse may be the ultimate prosody. It does, however, have limitations. The primary limitation is that it's harder to remember free verse than an end-rhymed, accentual-syllabic poetry. End-rhymed accentual-syllabic poetry, however, has its limitations too. The primary one is its inherently public character. As the Yeats passage might suggest, the public, oratorical quality of end-rhymed, accentual-syllabic verse may be incommensurable with the intimate quality of good free verse, its capacity to manifest a sense of individual "voice," though neither of the examples above of vers libre is very intimate. Their subject matter is impersonal: beauty. *In general, though, my sense is that the relative subjectivity of most modern poetry and its historical coincidence with the invention of free verse is no accident.*

The main advantage of end-rhymed accentual-syllabic verse is its memorability and its public character; the main advantage of free verse is its capacity to frame metaphors and to distill a medley of old prosodies. A third advantage of free verse is that it can take on mimetic tasks more easily than numerical prosodies can, though we are familiar with such famous examples in traditional prosody as Tennyson's "murmuring of innumerable bees" and Wilfred Owen's "Only the stuttering rifles' rapid rattle / Can patter out their hasty orisons." The most far-reaching justification of traditional prosody, though, is given by the Pulitzer prize–winning poet Robert Hillyer in his book *In Pursuit of Poetry*, where he argues that meter is natural, whereas free verse is not.

> Intricate though verse seems, it is a more natural form of expression than prose. Verse means a turning, and since the turn must come full circle on itself, we speak of it as repeating, or recurrent, rhythm, just as in music. Prose rhythm is non-recurrent; hence verse is more natural because it is closer to the rhythms of the universe—and note that *universe* means a concerted turning. . . . How foolish it is for defenders of free verse to maintain that . . . metrical structures are not natural. Free verse has no roots at all, and is itself an unnatural departure from the ebb and flow of all things.

Like a great deal of political rhetoric, this argument contains a grain of truth and then either misunderstands the implications of that truth or deliberately misuses it in order to reach an implausible conclusion. There are two misstatements in the passage: that "prose rhythm is non-recurrent" and that "free verse has no roots at all." There is no need to refute Hillyer's argument per se. We need only to adduce an example of free verse that, while it affirms Hillyer's conception of the periodic aspects of natural process, does so at least as persuasively as any numerical prosody could—does so *because* it is in free verse. Such a poem is "The Barn," by Wendell Berry. It affirms Hillyer's conception of the universe, but in a truly sophisticated way:

1. While we unloaded the hay from the truck, building
2. the great somnolence of the ricked bales, the weather
3. kept up its movement over us, the rain dashed and drove
4. against the roof, and in the close heat we sweated
5. to the end of the load. The fresh warm sweet smell
6. of new timothy in it, the barn is a nut ripened
7. in forethought of cold. Weighted now, it turns
8. toward the future generously, spacious
9. in its intent, the fledged young of the barn swallows
10. fluttering on the rim of the nest, the brown bats
11. hanging asleep, folded beneath the rafters.
12. And we rest, having done what men are best at.

As I have earlier suggested, the way to extract echoes of numerical prosodies from a passage of free verse is, first of all, to try to scan individual lines, then to try breaking the lines differently and scanning the result. Scansion of the original seems to yield no readily identifiable order, except that the last three lines have four strong stresses each, setting up the touch rhyme of "brown bats" (line 10) with "best at" (line 12).

Suppose we break the lines at the end of the most obvious syntactical units:

1. While we unloaded the hay from the truck,
2. building the great somnolence of the ricked bales,
3. the weather kept up its movement over us,
4. the rain dashed and drove against the roof,

5. and in the close heat we sweated to the end of the load.
6. The fresh warm sweet smell of timothy in it,
7. the barn is a nut ripened in forethought of cold.
8. Weighted now, it turns toward the future generously,
9. spacious in its intent.
10. the fledged young of the barn swallows
11. fluttering on the rim of the nest,
12. the brown bats hanging asleep,
13. folded, beneath the rafters. And we rest,
14. having done what men are best at.

In this version, the prosodic norm of the first eight syntactical units is that of tetrameter accentuals. Then a new norm—trimeter accentuals—replaces the tetrameter. Does the poem then consist of two prosodies, one after the other? Perhaps. But the tentative rhyme of "bats" in line 10 of the original suggests a more complex solution. Noticing that the sound of long *a* is conspicuously alliterated—"hay," "greater," "bales"—in the first two lines of the original, we wonder whether perhaps these "rhymes," like the rhyme of "rest" and "best," aren't also three stresses apart. And, indeed, if we break the lines of the original so that these long-*a* sounds fall at the ends of lines, those sounds become, in effect, end-rhymes to lines of trimeter:

1. While we unloaded the *hay*
2. from the truck, building the *great*
3. somnolence of the ricked *bales*
4. the weather kept up its movement
5. over us, the rain dashed
6. the drove against the roof,
7. and in the close *heat*
8. we sweated to the end of the *load*.
9. The fresh warm *sweet*
10. smell of new timothy in it,
11. the barn is a nut ripened
12. in forethought of *cold*.
13. Weighted now, it turns

14. toward the future generously,
15. spacious in its intent,
16. the fledged young of the barn swallows
17. fluttering on the rim of the nest,
18. the brown bats hanging asleep,
19. folded, beneath the rafters. And we rest,
20. having done what men are best at.

The trimeter version of "The Barn" immediately brings into the foreground other "rhymes" besides the long-a sounds: the rhyme of "heat" and "sweet" (which alliterates with "it" on line 10), and it brings into the foreground the alliteration of long o and d in "cold" and "load." We notice also that "nest" falls into line as an end-rhyme with "best." And suddenly we understand the strategy Berry, consciously or not, had been following all along. With the poem's last two words, "best at," the "nest-rest-best" end-rhyme expectations of the trimeter prosody coincide with the "bat-at" end-rhyme expectations set up by the pentameter at the end of the original version. The two prosodies, each of which echoes in counterpoint a different cycle—one a natural cycle, the other a human cycle—converge. Each autumn (the poem's setting), "men" and the "fledged young" of the natural world find themselves conducting activities that are "in forethought of cold": the curves of the two cycles, out of phase for the rest of the year, coincide. As Berry wrote in "The Specialization of Poetry":

> Song is natural; we have it in common with animals. It is also traditional . . . . Rhythm is fundamental to it, and is its profoundest reference. The rhythm of a song or poem rises, no doubt, in reference to the pulse and breath of the poet, as is often said, but that is still too specialized an accounting: it rises also in reference to daily and seasonal—and surely even longer—rhythms in the life of the poet and in the life that surrounds him. The rhythm of a poem resonates with these larger rhythms that surround it; it fills its environment with sympathetic vibrations. Rhyme, which is a function of rhythm, may suggest this sort of resonance; it marks the coincidences of the

rhythm of the structure with the rhyme of the lines, or the coincidences of small structures with larger ones, as when the day, the month, and the year all end at the same moment.

The free-verse line may be the most sensitive prosodic instrument available for registering and dramatizing these coincidences, because in the hands of poets of Berry's and Voigt's skill it is tied to traditional echoes which, in turn, are profoundly rooted in the cyclical aspects of natural process. As Berry puts it: "Song, then, is a force opposed to specialty and isolation. It is the testimony of the singer's inescapable relation to the world, to human community, and also, I think, to tradition." Or, as Eliot had written, "No verse is free for the man [or woman] who wants to do a good job."

II

PERSONAE

Leonard Nathan

Poet as Odysseus

WE HAVE BEEN discussing the character of the poetic persona, the issue of authenticity, and the moral authority of poetry and the poet. In the spring 1998 issue of *Prairie Schooner*, the "special poetry issue," poet Ted Kooser led off with a short essay entitled "Lying for the Sake of Making Poems." Kooser wrote:

> Perhaps I am hopelessly old-fashioned. Perhaps I should accept the possibility that what the poet says happened really didn't happen at all; but I'm going to have to make a painful adjustment in the way I read poetry and honor poets. I grew up believing a lyric poet was a person who wrote down his or her observations taken from life. I have always trusted the "I" of Walt Whitman as he dresses the wounds of the fallen soldiers; . . . When "I" says something happened, I believe it happened.

Or, as I put it in my introduction to this book, I think that poetry should be read "naively." What I propose now is to give you my reading of ten poets. These are all poets I have admired and studied, and I would like them to be understood as I understand them. None of them has been read well enough.

The first of these is Leonard Nathan, whose poetry I have always loved, not just because he is good but because his approach to poetry is like mine, in that he has always seen poetry as a form of rhetoric. My first critical book was titled *The Rhetoric of the Contemporary Lyric* (1980), and in it I wrote:

> Although I am quite aware that the term "rhetoric" no longer refers

to the art if oratory but refers more to "style," I still tend to regard rhetoric as having something to do with persuasion; and, unfashionable as it may seem, I have used it in roughly this way . . . If "rhetoric" is traditionally "the art of persuasion," then, whenever we consider the way in which a poet or novelist might have tried to anticipate and play upon the expectations and the disposition of his audience, we are considering the rhetorical aspects of a work of imaginative literature. To narrow my usage further: Throughout these essays the rhetorical aspects of a poem or any piece of literature are those that touch on the issue of who is speaking to whom, through what mask, and for what ostensible purpose.

To some extent, Nathan's poems can be regarded, like the cantatas of Johann Sebastian Bach, as exercises in practical rhetoric. His poetry is conspicuously innovative in significant ways, and his poems, though highly sophisticated, are accessible to the literate nonspecialist. Yet Nathan's achievement has received nowhere near the wide recognition it deserves.

The poems in *Carrying On*, Nathan's new and selected poems, comprise a persuasive vision of the world, a vision that would be bleak if not for the fierceness of Nathan's energy and the accuracy of his wit. The poems are unified by the character of their author, a character whose style, as we watch it evolve over time, reflects changes in fashion but also the inevitable changes of an individual aging. Like Odysseus, his life story is an exemplum for us. We can watch him passing through aesthetic initiations, academic initiations, political initiations, and personal initiations. The scenery is continuously changing; but the underlying character of the poet, who is brilliant and restless, driven by his daemon, fascinates us. We can watch as we might watch the main character in a good novel, say Richard Ford's Frank Bascombe in *The Sportswriter* or its sequel, *Independence Day*. We look to him, for all his imperfections, for guidance. He is a version of us.

Nathan has made his life as a professor of rhetoric at the University of California, Berkeley, and in his poems his rhetorical training is clearly and fortuitously evident. What distinguishes his poems from those of his contemporaries is Nathan's rhetorical calculation—his consciousness of audience. Few of the poems are "lyric" in the sense of featuring a speaker who, as Northrop Frye put it in his *Anatomy of Criticism*, has turned his back to the audience, intending that his inner meditations be "overheard": Nathan generally faces the reader directly. Typical of his early poetic style and its rhetorical tactics would be his elegant "The Loophole" from *The Day the Perfect Speakers Left* (Wesleyan, 1969). It begins:

> Any contract, tax form, Great Idea,
> Existentialist brick wall,
> Or even the cloudless air provides
> Some saving orifice after all,
> Through which, well greased, the lawyer, the statesman,
> Or the fattest theologian can squeeze.

Nathan then, in a move characteristic of him, addresses the audience:

> But you're on the proper side, of course.
> Some have heard voices from that world—
> Distorted, wishful, uttering facts
> Terrible in their lack of portent:
> Anyone's name (say, John) or acts,
> Like loving when it seems to open
> The ivory gates for you alone,
> But closes, after sex is finished,
> On something alien as stone.

Facing "The Loophole" is "The Day the Perfect Speakers Left," a poem reminiscent of Richard Wilbur's "Merlin Enthralled." The Wilbur poem is about the passing of magic (and medieval superstition) from the world, leaving that world simply quaint, the sky "a still and woven blue." In Nathan's version, this passing is reminiscent of Stevens's "Sunday Morning":

> Their words are hard to say, hard
> To remember when you wake at dawn,
> The bare light alerting you to plainness,
> Solitude of stones, terror in birds,
> Stars drifting off, the feel of huge leave-takings

For which no name, the first or last, consoles.
How can you trust those hints at dusk
Of foreign magnificence.

Just as Nathan's earlier collections, with their wit, their frequent
end-rhyming, and their impersonality had reflected the Eliotian late-
modernist style of the fifties, *Returning Your Call* (1975) reflects the pressure
of the confessional style of that literary-historical moment. Nathan does
not, however, except for the first poem, get sloppy and overpersonal. The
"you" of *Your Call* is a figure that is at once a lover, Nathan's mother, a
muse, and, of course, the reader—the audience of which Nathan is ever
conscious. But the opening poem, "Breathing Exercises," which features
the first-person-singular pronoun, is panicky sounding, even a little
whining:

> My mother phoning from far off:
> How are you? Are you really? Really?
>
> A long dumbness fills with breathing.
> How much does she want to know? Really?
>
> I'm fine, fighting, making passes,
> Doing my job. Does that sound right?
>
> No, it sounds as if somebody bugged
> The phone and I'm talking for the bugger,
> Which reminds me: I'm Leonard Nathan whose grandpa
>
> Changed his last name—too Jewish.

The dominant feel of the book is of grim, personal crisis—of a man
struggling to retain equilibrium in the face of marital crisis and public
crisis: the Vietnam War. In the book's best poem, "Washing Socks," he
compares himself to Odysseus:

> Penelope, old dear, you write
> That all that keeps you sane these days
> Is washing socks, faded socks,
> And add: "For godsake, come on home."

I'm out here having adventures, sleeping
With goddesses, though sometimes I feel
Like a swine. I'm battling giant man-
Eating abstractions. I'm at sea.

There was the island of Romance, the greener
Islands of Marx, of Freud, the misty
Isle of Zen and the volcanic Sartre.
And then there is plain old Ithaca.

"The Penance" is perhaps Nathan's grimmest poem, linking his sense
of personal suffering to the spectacle of suffering in the Vietnam War. It
begins by describing a famous piece of TV documentary footage:

This is the penance: a recurring dream,
The child running down the road, its mouth
A hole filled up with blackness, its little wings
Two flares of napalm and it runs toward you. . . .

Now you hear its scream—a supersonic
jet-like whine that peels your skin off patch
By patch, and then the face is in your face,
Close as a lover's, eyes as bleak as bullets. . . .
So this is the penance: a recurring dream
That you're awake and doing good, loving
The children, saving for their education
And your own retirement—till you close your eyes.

In the final poem, "Audit," a poem that recalls the ending of Roethke's
"The Lost Son," Nathan describes the tentative beginnings of recovery:

The year is done. There are certain things against you.
The lull is around the house, waiting.
But moss on the cold side of the bark is with you.
A jackrabbit frozen at the odor of fox is with you,
And a last apple, with a worm in it. . . .
On the north side of this thought, the moss is ready
To fend off the wind; or you breathe, and the wind is with you.

When Returning Your Call was published, Nathan was fifty-two years old. It's grimness may be characteristic of collections by men in their late forties and early fifties—this sense of the direness of human existence. When men pass through such a season, though, they are apt to emerge with a sense of playfulness, the ability to regard their lives *sub specie aeternitatis*. *Dear Blood* (1980) begins with a Zen-like poem entitled "Gap":

> This is the gap
> for one butterfly to pass through,
> a lucky break in the senseless green.
>
> It's there by the grace of God,
> who I think is the absence of a spider
> at this particular time and place.
>
> You may think He's the absence only
> of leaves now dead or, more incredible yet,
> the presence of the one butterfly.

The poem's tone of wonderment and tentative acceptance of things as they are is reminiscent of Eliot's "Mariana." In Nathan's poem "Opportunity," we watch him revise the existentialist posture that had so thoroughly informed his earlier work.

> We thought we owned the apple
> having raised it simply
> to bite at our pleasure.
>
> But this worm
> found it a sweet way
> into its own ripeness.
>
> That was a mouthful
> of sour knowledge
> for spitting out.
> Could there be a higher purpose
> that used us both
> toward its own ripening?
>
> Ha, say the dark seeds,
> ha, and exult
> to the core.

In "Family Circle," Nathan again compares his life to that of Odysseus and concludes by embracing home and domesticity:

> When I left Ithaca
> for the great action
> I was clean-cut . . .
> Well, here I am finally,
> beat-up pilgrim to a homely shrine,
> my bare rock and old woman
> willing glumly to receive what I offer—
> a scar and a tall story.
>
> I see my son's eyes lift slyly
> from his plate, asking what it was for—
> struggle, shipwreck, and such lies.
> It was for this, sonny, this:
> my eating and your asking.

Holding Patterns (1982) marks a significant advance in Nathan's poetry and contains some of his best poems: extended meditations that have a narrative quality and which feature a "He" and a "She." The epistemology of the book is dictated by its opening poem, "The Understanding," which dismisses realism, ending: "Language is just / music to live by anyway." The book then, in the three longish poems that make up its heart, presents characters meditating on religious experiences. "Meadow Foam," a poem that bears significant similarities to Stevens's "The Idea of Order at Key West," begins with an epiphany revealed to a man walking with his wife beside the ocean.

> The afternoon
> hundreds of blackbirds
> suddenly sprang up
> out of the cedars of the cemetery
> he felt, for Christ's sake,
> a vision had been vouchsafed
> the wrong man again,

The blackbird epiphany touches off various memories, longings, reflections,

             flagrant visions
         that seem to hint of Great Doings
         behind the masks of mere light
         and shadow, . . .
         he stood looking for a word
         that would let him be—say, "reconciled,"
         spoken with good-humored sadness

"Without thinking" he turns "to the woman beside him," a woman with
"gray hair that hung / in thin bangs across her forehead." He muses:

             there's your love
         for you, the fine art of charity
         and tact, of noticing and not
         noticing, for example, people,
         the world, or little scenes in it

He reflects on death and his own heart, "the same old faithful pump /
fifty-eight years serving it knew / not what, perhaps the vague hunger /
they used to call the soul." His reflections return to the blackbird
epiphany, to

         . . . the way common blackbirds crash
         into an almost acceptable scene
         to distract the comfortably disappointed
         from their little faith,
         or even simpler, as when she knelt
         last Sunday morning by the sea,
         knelt at what he hadn't noticed
         just at his feet, a white surprise
         or wild flower out of its place,
         time, maybe even its world,
         knelt . . . and . . .
         repeated like an unanswerable prayer
         for all things that must stand for themselves, . . .
         "meadow-foam, oh meadow-foam,
         of course," and that would have to do.

This concluding epiphany, like the famous one in Joyce's *Portrait of the Artist*, is proposing art as religion: "and that would have to do."

This passage illustrates an aspect of Nathan's later poetry that, to my mind, is of particular significance: the marshalling of an extended, elaborated, almost Jamesian sentence syntax that is not so much a means of adjusting degrees of assertiveness and qualification in a poem's statements as it is a rhetorical method of *inventio*. But the word *method* is inexact. Nathan's sentence syntax extends beyond method. It is a principle of poetic form (though I would prefer the word *structure*). To say, as I happen to believe, that the structure of a poem *is* its sentence syntax is to risk stating a truism, but one that is not quite as obvious as it might first appear. In Nathan's best poems, sentence syntax is intricately and knowingly woven into the poem's statement. To view free-verse sentence structure deployed this way, I invite the reader to read Nathan's "Table Talk," a poem of 109 lines that is all one sentence, a sentence so cunningly strung out that it seems to imitate the poet's mind itself at work, weighing, measuring, sorting, musing, all with "good-humored sadness" while evoking, from the limited third-person point of view, the soul of a middle-aged woman:

> She was just about to say,
> through the candles and over the wine,
> with the oak table and so much else
> between them, that distance
> was no less fine an invention
> than the wheel, but didn't
> because his smile was too far off,
> so asked softly instead: Are you there?
> and knew, though he lifted his glass
> to her, he wasn't, but somewhere back
> in himself alone with something dearer
> to him than any woman now,
> what—for modesty—he called
> his disappointment, that is, failure,
> which these days left her much

> to herself to decide just who
> she was after all these years
> typecast as daughter, wife, mother,
> double agent in the lost war
> of the sexes, or someone . . .

Poems like this are as revolutionary (and successful) as the early narrative poems of Robert Frost. When I encountered them in journals, they so disturbed me that I ordered *Carrying On* from Pitt Press. They were like good novels in miniature, like movies. The personae in these poems, like the characters in Woody Allen's serious films, such as *September* and *Interiors*, haunted me with their desires. They seemed to live, like all of us, in the suspense of imminent disappointment. The reader compares his or her life to theirs. This is their intended effect, their "argument," but to label such an appeal a rhetorical "tactic" or "method" would demean them. So deeply is their human sympathy woven into their syntax, their "Holding Patterns," that it would be more appropriate to speak of "strategy" rather than tactics. "Tactics" issue from technique; "strategy" is the result of vision.

It is through such strategic vision that the best poems in the thirty-eight pages of "New Poems" conspire to hurt the reader. Nathan has never stood still as a poet. His work has continuously improved. He has experimented. He has taken nothing for granted. Perhaps the most appropriate way to close this appreciation might be to tease the reader with the beginning of Nathan's "Twin Snakes," a poem about boxing and about stardom—its temptations and its costs. As I mentioned at the beginning of this piece, Nathan's achievement has received nowhere near the recognition that it deserves, and this fact—a fact of which Nathan is well aware—may underlie the poignancy of the poem. Nathan can imagine stardom all too well:

> Always for money, yes, and, yes,
> to hurt whoever stood there waiting,
> a reach away, to hurt him,
> and yes, for the looks he got
> by winning—cold admiration

in the eyes of women, even
his mother's— yes, for all that
and something more he couldn't say
but *was* the night he stood, radiant
with sweat, over a leathery man
he'd put down for the final time
and saw, like a vapor or spirit lifting
up from the smeared and slack stare
of the beaten other, recognition,
a swelling power that filled him
as his own hands filled the gloves
he held high over his head,
the same hands some fool of a writer
had called all flash and blur,
another, twin snakes, yes,
the crowd chanting "Snake! Snake!"
as the police slowly wedged him back
toward his dressing room through waves
of fingers reaching to touch or snatch
a piece of him or his power,
and yes, after, out there
on the blurred and flashing street,
the girl on his arm, almost sick
with privilege, looking up to moan,
"You a *God!*" and he laughed, ashamed
for her, but knew he was, knew
he could make things be by thinking them,
be here: his ex-wife glittering
with regret, the blonde actress
who loved only the best, and then
the party in the rich hotel
where an old champion came up
and hugged him, whispering in his ear,
"I know," then stepped back, his arms
still wide, his suit too big,
his face gray as a man's a storm
has passed through or a fatal illness
badly survived.

Next morning,
his own face woke him crying
out its hurt, but the girl slept on
as if she had shared the bed with just
another man, and when he opened
the morning papers it was like reading
of someone else.

The dream of stardom: it is impossible, living in America, not to wistfully fantasize about stardom. It is not unlike an addiction—a minor one—and it is deeply American. It is a luxurious addiction. Whereas Nathan's persona in his earlier poems was sometimes like that of Odysseus, in his later poems it appears to be the man, Leonard Nathan himself. It is the measure of Nathan's character that he can view the entire story of his selves with such knowingness and compasssion. Such knowingness is the implicit subject of Nathan's later poems. Another word for it is wisdom.

Ted Kooser

The Chekhov of American Poetry

IN HIS LATEST poetry collection, *Weather Central*, Ted Kooser continues
to turn out the kind of short lyric of which he is the undisputed master;
but here, as in his previous collections with Pitt Press, *Sure Signs* (1980)
and *One World at a Time* (1985), Kooser produces far more than a collection
of beautiful little poems. His writing is reminiscent of the short stories
of Anton Chekhov. Chekhov, we remember, was (amid his several lives) a
country doctor. In fact (as is well known), the tuberculosis which Chekhov
eventually died from was the result of his making constant treks to the
Russian hinterland to treat the rural poor, long before the invention of
antibiotics. Chekhov was a man attentive to his people, and there is a
similar nurturing attentiveness to "local" people in Kooser's poetry—
a humanitarian vision. Indeed, Kooser might well be regarded as a kind
of country doctor to his community—there to help them recognize the
beauty around them, to record the seasons for them, to keep a sort of
quiet almanac of their lives and deaths; for, like Chekhov's writing,
Kooser's writing is the result of a coherent vision not only of people
dwelling together in a particular place but of the place itself. Like
Chekhov's stories, the human relevance of Kooser's poems extends far
beyond his "village." It is universal.

In art, the proof of the pudding is always in the tasting. Great art has
many properties: structural beauty, memorability, enticing surfaces. But
if, as with Kooser, the art is a realist art, a sine qua non is that it be accurate. Consider the following passage for its accuracy:

In Late Spring

One of the National Guard's F-4 fighters,
making a long approach to the Lincoln airfield,
comes howling in over the treetops, its shadow
flapping along behind it like the skin of a sheep,
setting the coyotes crying back in the woods,
and then the dogs, and then there is a sudden quiet

that rings a little, the way an empty pan
rings when you wipe it dry, and then it is
Sunday again, a summer Sunday afternoon,
and beyond my window, the Russian olives
sigh foolishly into the air through the throats of their flowers,
and bluegills nibble the clouds afloat on the pond.

Under the windmill, a cluster of peonies huddles,
bald-headed now. . . .

Always Kooser is recording the events of an entire community.

Like Chekhov, Kooser notices people, too. Indeed, it is perhaps Kooser's interest in people other than himself which sets his poems both apart from and above the poems of virtually all of his contemporaries. Here is an example, "Four Secretaries":

All through the day I hear or overhear
their clear, light voices calling
from desk to desk, young women whose fingers
play casually over their documents,

setting the incoming checks to one side,
the thick computer reports to the other,
tapping the correspondence into stacks
while they sing to each other, not intending

to sing nor knowing how beautiful
their voices are as they call back and forth,
singing their troubled marriage ballads,
their day-care, car-park, landlord songs.

Even their anger with one another
is lovely: the color rising in their throats,
their white fists clenched in their laps,
the quiet between them that follows.

And their sadness—how deep and full of love
is their sadness when one among them
is hurt, and they hear her calling
and gather about her to cry.

The clarity of Kooser's vision in this poem reminds me of an anthropologist marveling at the collective behavior of a tribe. The poem is dangerously close to being sentimental; but, as Richard Hugo wrote in *The Triggering Town*, "If you don't risk sentimentality, you're not in the ballpark." The word *beautiful* as used here by Kooser has approximately the same meaning as it does in the poems of William Carlos Williams, where *beautiful* is a metaphor for that which is so startlingly real that, in its blemishes, it borders on ugliness. *Beautiful* for both Kooser and Williams means something like "authentic." Kooser is endlessly fascinated with the epistemological conditions of authenticity.

Great poetry, like Kooser's, like Chekhov's stories, is not sentimental, but it is characterized by a kind of tender wisdom communicated with absolute precision; for example, Kooser's poem "In Passing," which describes passing somebody who seems vaguely familiar on the street and not being able to decide whether or not to acknowledge them:

From half a block off I see you coming,
walking briskly along, carrying parcels,
furtively glancing up into faces
of people approaching, looking for someone
you know, holding your smile in your mouth
like a pebble, keeping it moist and ready,
being careful not to swallow.

. . .

From a few feet away, you recognize me,
or think you do. I see you preparing your face,

getting your greeting ready. Do I know you?
Both of us wonder. Swiftly we meet and pass,
averting our eyes, close enough to touch,
but not touching. I could not let you know
that I've forgotten, and yet you know.

Thank heavens not all the poems in *Weather Central* are this good; a few
indulge, almost by reflex and a bit too mechanically, in the personifications that are the signature of Kooser's style. But a few of the poems here,
though short, are truly major poems. Poems like "Some Kinds of Love"
and "Another Story" transcend all the usual categories. In them, as in all
of Kooser's work, we view people going about their lives in a landscape;
but these poems have a quiet weight that is truly unusual, because it is
unforced. It is not rhetorical. Such poems are equal to the best poems of
Thomas Hardy, poems like Hardy's "In Time of 'The Breaking of Nations,' "
with its famous ending: "Yonder a maid and her wight / Come whispering by; / War's annals will cloud into night / Ere their story die."

In "Another Story," the landscape and its figures could be in Hardy's
"Wessex," in Nebraska, or in the Ukraine. The poem is in the past tense,
giving it a kind of monumentality, viewing its figures *sub specie aeternitatis*:

In a country churchyard, two workmen
were digging a grave. It was summer,
but cool in the cedar-blue shade
of the white clapboard church where they labored.

Their picks did all of the talking.
Beyond them, a field of tall corn
glittered with heat, and above, a lone bird
rose on the air like an ash.

The grave grew slowly down
and out of the world, and the world rolled
under the work. Then the men stopped.
One stooped to scrape in the clay.

When he stood, light-headed,
swaying a little, he held in his hand

an old cowbell, covered with dirt
and packed with darkness.

He scraped out the earth with his knife.
The bell had no clapper. He shook it.
A meadowlark piped on a fence post.
In the distance, a feeder thunked.

He handed it across the grave
to the younger man, who held it in his hands
like a baby bird, then rang it tenderly.
A crow cawed in a cedar top.

He rang it again, On the highway,
a mile away, a semi trumpeted.
In the cornfield, an irrigation pump
thumped with a regular heartbeat.

He handed it back to the older man,
who set it aside. All afternoon,
they worked without a word between them.
At intervals each touched the empty bell.

"At intervals." Though the poem doesn't mention music, the men's lives *are* music. And the poem is music transcribed—the symphony of the community—in which Kooser's final line is a note of genius.

Ted Kooser is, like Anton Chekhov, a kind of healer. The character of the persona of his poetry is the man himself, and the community knows it. This character is, without asserting himself, exemplary. He simply demonstrates, in poem after poem, the possibilities of moral authority in poetry. But there are as many different kinds of character as there are people in the world. Let us examine some more "types"—the first a kind of scapegoat; the second a poet as clown; the third an intellectual living guardedly in a half-savage country; the fourth an intellectual mother who, knowing the temptations of authenticity, is horrified by her own knowingness; the last a famous poet/editor grappling with breast cancer.

Richard Hugo's Gift to Us
The Permission for Emotional Honesty

I REMEMBER IN 1980, when Richard Hugo read at Kansas State in the preternaturally ugly room of Denison 123. The building's thermostat was broken. The air temperature in Denison Hall was above eighty degrees. Hugo began by talking. Heavy, troll-like, he stumped back and forth before the front row seats, yakking in a loud, guffawing yet oddly confidential way about growing up poor, when he was raised by his grandmother Ora Monk.

Marbles of sweat began to form on his face and roll down. But his talk had crossed a threshold, become more organized, and I realized that he was reciting from memory, as though still talking, "What Thou Lovest Well Remains American," and we were gripped in the enhancements of art, by the subtle exaggerations that make up true style. He could have gone on for hours, and we would have sat there.

That may not be true anymore. Confessional poetry is no longer fashionable. It was invented in the late sixties and early seventies—a reaction to what Robert Lowell called "the tranquilized fifties." But the zeitgeist has changed. Daytime television, shows such as the *Jerry Springer Show*, have replaced poetry as the preferred venue of public confession, and poetry has withdrawn somewhat. As I have already mentioned, this is a salutary trend in poetry. Outrageous honesty is no longer endorsed, carte blanche, as a sign of good character. Many of us, perhaps because we are older, or perhaps because we are disappointed in the results of "emotional honesty," are now more cautious and more particular than we used to be. The spectacle of "confessional" poetry has begun to seem almost quaint.

95

Nevertheless, both it and the career of Richard Hugo are still worth reassessing.

One of Richard Hugo's earliest published poems, written, according to the poet, "eleven or twelve years before my first book was accepted for publication," is "West Marginal Way." This would date its composition in 1948 or 1949, when he was twenty-five. A veteran of World War II, he was then living with his grandparents in relatively impoverished circumstances in White Center, on the outskirts of Seattle, and majoring in creative writing at the University of Washington. Early as this poem is in Hugo's canon, it displays virtually all the significant features of his best and most characteristic later work. It reads:

> One tug pounds to haul an afternoon
> of logs up river. The shade
> of Pigeon Hill across the bulges
> in the concrete crawls on reeds
> in a short field, cools a pier
> and the violence of young men
> after cod. The crackpot chapel,
> with a sign erased by rain, returned
> before to calm and a mossed roof.
>
> A dim wind blows the roses
> growing where they please. Lawns
> are wild and lots are undefined
> as if the payment made in cash
> were counted then and there.
>
> These names on boxes will return
> with salmon money in the fall,
> come drunk down the cinder arrow
> of a trail, past the store of Popich,
> sawdust piles and the saw mill
> bombing air with optimistic sparks,
> blinding gravel pits and the brickyard
> baking, to wives who taught themselves
> the casual thirst of many summers
> wet in heat and taken by the sea.

Some places are forever afternoon.
Across the road and a short field
there is the river, split and yellow
and this far down affected by the tide.

Like so many of Hugo's poems, "West Marginal Way" is a landscape poem, richly descriptive, depicting a small community, village, or town. Here the village is Riverside, a community near White Center, which Hugo wrote about in his autobiographical essay "The Real West Marginal Way":

I first became aware of Riverside as a community when I was thirteen, starting high school. . . . Going home I would wait at the bus stop in the rundown grocery owned by two Greeks. . . .West Marginal Way started south from there. . . . A cinder walk paralleled it down to the Riverside community at the bottom of the hill. Although the village was made up of drab frame houses, in layout it was more European than any other community in Seattle. The houses seemed jammed together giving the total village some definition. Some houses were flush against West Marginal Way with no yard separating them from cars that passed a few feet away. . . . Many immigrants lived there and the names were exotic: Vokov, Zuvela, Zitkovich. The place always seemed beautiful to me. A big field covered by sawdust lay east between West Marginal Way and the Duwamish River where Riverside boys fished for cod.

The Riverside of "West Marginal Way" typifies the sort of setting that time and again Hugo used in his poetry—places that are backwaters, poor and conspicuously rundown yet rich in local color, places that exhibit what Hugo would later call "style," his word for beauty, the kind of aesthetic authenticity that is often associated with celebrated ruins. But Hugo's ruins are usually not European, and they are not listed in travel brochures, nor do they possess any orthodox aesthetic value like the Parthenon. They are, instead, a domestic variety of ruins—played-out mining towns, poor, backward mill towns all covered with a patina of dust, stagnation, defeat, and a sense that history has passed them by—landscapes with the same aura of desolation yet nostalgia that we see in the paintings of Edward Hopper and Andrew Wyeth.

Although Hugo grew up near Riverside, in the poem "West Marginal Way," as in each of his landscape poems, the speaker's relation to the landscape is that of an outsider—a sort of poetic tourist—able to reconstruct from the visible evidence of ruin the cramped lives of the inhabitants, able through his extreme sensitivity to evoke the somber mood of stalemate that is the genius of the place. We watch the poet construct a little myth in which he makes himself at home in the landscape, asking himself—and the reader—What would it feel like to have one's home here? The fictive life that "West Marginal Way" extrapolates would be stagnant, heavy with a sense of monotonous repetition—tide, season, weather, daily labor—and little if any forward progress. The tug "pounds to haul an afternoon / of logs up river"; but the effort is immense and wearying, and the tug hardly gets anywhere. So static, so paralyzed is the landscape that the poet begins to notice such subtle and insignificant details as how the shade of "Pigeon Hill" changes the appearance of the water and "cools" a pier. What little activity there is stands out: the "optimistic sparks" of the mill, the "dim wind," and the nearly imperceptible changes of the tide. The river is not fresh and blue but "yellow," and the mention of "the tide" closes the poem on a note of profound longing and sadness. The polluted yellow river seeks the blue freedom of the ocean; but only the faintest intimation of that freedom—the effect of the tide—reaches inland to this place, a scene which is a landscape of Hugo's imagined sense of his own paralysis. Indeed, this landscape, we feel, is intended not merely as a metaphor to describe the speaker's felt inner life. It is offered as a confirmation of it. By singling out the appropriate evidence, he has justified his own predicament. He has found not just an "objective correlative" for his misery, but a sort of company for it. He has constructed a myth—a version of the world—that both accounts for and defines the present unsatisfactory condition of his inner life. According to this myth, his condition is the authentic condition of the world.

Is such a projection of the poet's inner life upon a landscape simply a backward-looking example of the now outmoded Pathetic Fallacy? Is "West Marginal Way" an example of what the critic Marjorie Perloff has dismissed as "instant Wordsworth?" In its treatment of the poet's sensibility as the main subject of the poem, "West Marginal Way" certainly belongs to a late stage of the tradition we label Romantic. But there are significant differences between the kind of myth making we see in Hugo's poems and the Pathetic Fallacy. For one thing, "West Marginal Way" contains—unless one wants to stretch a point and call "optimistic sparks" personification—no personifications. Nor do we feel that the operation of imagination on the scene was, as Wordsworth would have prescribed, prompted by "passion" occasioning "a spontaneous overflow of powerful feelings." Instead, we are conscious of a *hypothetical* quality to the poem's suppositions: "as if the payment made in cash / were counted then and there." The poem seems not so much the dramatization of a definitive vision as of a proposal. Hence it stands on the page as only a *version*, a tentative one, of the poet's self.

In its proposal of a given landscape as a version of the poet's self, "West Marginal Way" is an early example of a way of writing that Hugo was to describe years later in his essay "Writing Off the Subject":

> A poem can be said to have two subjects, the initiating or triggering subject, which starts the poem or "causes" the poem to be written, and the real or generated subject, which the poem comes to say or mean, and which is generated or discovered in the poem during the writing. . . .
>
> I suspect that the true or valid triggering subject is one in which physical characteristics or details correspond to attitudes the poet has toward the world and himself. For me, a small town that has seen better days often works. . . . I would never try to locate a serious poem in a place where physical evidence suggests that the people there find it relatively easy to accept themselves—say the new Hilton.

What Hugo calls "the real or generated subject" bears a similar relationship to the "triggering subject" as (according to psychoanalytic theory) the latent content of a dream bears to that dream's manifest content. The generated subject is a version of the poet's self, a self that can only be approached obliquely, by indirection—by a procedure that (as Hugo describes it) is strikingly similar to the psychoanalytic technique of free association. The poem is like a waking dream encouraged into being by the "dreamer," who must trust the poem to exhibit its own coherence and authenticity. In the words of Hugo:

> Don't be afraid to jump ahead. . . . Make the subject of the next sentence different from the subject you just put down. Depend on rhythm, tonality, and the music of language to hold things together. It is impossible to write meaningless sequences. In a sense the next thing always belongs.

The "triggering town" serves, in effect, the same function as a Rorschach inkblot: it initiates a process of free association. In order to maximize freedom of association—of imagination—it is naturally best, Hugo advises, to choose a "place" about which "you know almost nothing of substance. . . . Knowing can be a limiting thing." The resulting process of composition is akin to a process of self-psychoanalysis:

> You have found the town, now you must start the poem. If the poem turns out good, the town will have become your hometown no matter what name it carries. It will accommodate those intimate hunks of self that could live only in your hometown. But you may have found those hunks of self because the externals of the triggering town you used were free of personal association and were that much easier to use.

A good example of Hugo's fully developed, self-conscious application of this technique is "Montesano Unvisited," a poem composed nearly twenty years after "West Marginal Way," a poem in which Hugo, having returned from a year spent in Italy to settle in Montana, reconstructs one of the triggering sites of his Italian trip:

> With houses hung that slanted and remote
> the road that goes there if you found it
> would be dangerous and dirt. Dust would cake
> the ox you drive by and you couldn't meet
> the peasant stare that drills you black. Birds

might be at home but rain would feel rejected
in the rapid drain and wind would bank off
fast without friend to stars. Inside
the convent they must really mean those prayers.

You never find the road. You pass the cemetery,
military, British, World War Two and huge.
Maybe your car will die and the garage
you go to will be out of parts. The hotel
you have to stay in may have postcard shots,
deep focus stuff, a grave close up
and far off, just as clear, the bright town
that is someone's grave. Towns are bad things happening,
a spear elected mayor, a whip ordained.
You know in that town there's a beautiful girl
you'd rescue if your horse could run.

When your car is fixed you head on north
sticking with the highway, telling yourself
if you'd gone it would have been no fun.
Mountain towns are lovely, hung way away
like that, throbbing in light. But stay in one
two hours. You pat your car and say
let's go, friend. You drive off never hearing
the bruised girl in the convent screaming
take me with you. I am not a nun.

On the literal level, what is happening here? The narrator, a hypothetical
male "you" riding around like a cowboy knight-errant in a car, is looking for an elusive mountain town that he might aesthetically "rescue."
He misses the turn he should have taken. His car breaks down, and he
has to spend the night in a strange hotel while his car is fixed. The next
morning he abandons the mission. Although he had been attracted to the
place—"Mountain towns are lovely"—the life he imagines living there
would be unbearable, like life in a convent, "a whip ordained." The dull,
stark life of repression and guilt that he imagines in Montesano reflects,
in part, Hugo's mythologized version of his own impoverished child-
hood in White Center, but some of the autobiography buried in the poem

is far more specific. The aborted rescue is a cryptic reflection of Hugo's feelings of guilt at the disintegration of his first marriage, which occurred while he and his wife, Barbara, were in Italy. The "nun" whom he feels he should have rescued is Barbara.

By symbolically equating her psychic isolation with a remote mountain location, Hugo employs a metaphor that he will later, in 31 *Letters and* 13 *Dreams,* apply to himself, to his own solipsism. The failure of the car/ horse to "run" is a metaphoric admission by Hugo of his own psychological limitations, and the healing process of a night's sleep, during which time the protagonist's psyche, through unconscious processes, comes to terms with reality, is a motif that recurs regularly in Hugo's signal poems, most notably in "The Lady in Kicking Horse Reservoir." When Hugo awakens, his car "fixed," he can accept his failure to rescue Barbara; he can, with relative equanimity, drive on, though not without a sense of compassion. The likening of the neglected town to a "convent" and the blunt statement "Towns are bad things happening" are reminders by Hugo that both he and Barbara had been raised in unhappy, repressive homes.

It would be wrong, of course, to read "Montesano Unvisited" as a piece of cryptic soap opera. One can appreciate it sufficiently without knowing its autobiographical background. The poem can be construed quite satisfactorily as a piece of evocative travelogue, about the transformation by the poetic imagination of a given setting. But the poem's real emotional energy is derived from the autobiographical context that is left implicit. "Montesano Unvisited" is therefore paradoxical. It reproduces accurately the emotional tone of Hugo's inner life as that life was connected with his separation from his first wife—his ambivalence, his guilt, his compassion—along with a newly discovered expectation of autonomy and freedom of movement. Yet it conceals the actual facts of the matter, presenting an aesthetic myth instead of autobiography. Painful autobiographical facts and a sense of personal failure have been reworked into an art object, converted into aesthetic victory.

It is a familiar story. One thinks of the country-and-western songs of George Jones, in which he recounts his heavy drinking and his failed marriage with Tammy Wynette. (Hugo is the George Jones of our poetry.) One thinks of the way in which most prominent artists in show business allow their personal lives to be displayed shamelessly. One thinks of the early "confessional" poets, such as Sylvia Plath, Anne Sexton, Robert Lowell, and W. D. Snodgrass. Hugo's oeuvre is beginning to look dated, though The Triggering Town remains a popular book in university creative writing programs.

Hugo was a self-indulgent writer, deriving his permission from the zeitgeist, during the creative writing boom of the 1970s, when every single college and university had to have its own creative-writing specialist, a time when, as Hugo put it in his "Letter to Levertov," America was a place "where enough money floats to the top for the shipwrecked / to hang on." Making Certain It Goes On, Hugo's collected poems from Norton, is a preposterously self-indulgent book: over four hundred pages of poems that repeat themselves, both thematically and in their iambic cadences, to the point of monotony. But of course: they were generated by formula. Meanwhile, in the late nineties, as we observe what economists coldly refer to as "the shake-out," Hugo's stock has fallen in value.

Nevertheless, Richard Hugo wrote a few great poems, most notably "Degrees of Gray in Philipsburg," that are going to survive. Or the lines from his early poem "Duwamish":

> On the short days, looking for a word,
> knowing the smoke from the small homes
> turns me colder than the wind from
> the cold river, knowing this poverty
> is not a lack of money but of friends,
> I come here to be cold. Not silver cold
> like ice, for ice has glitter. Gray cold
> like the river. Cold like 4 P.M.
> on Sunday. Cold like a decaying porgy.

"Gray cold / like the river. Cold like 4 P.M. / on Sunday." These are words which the lonely and the disfranchised can turn to for a kind of comfort. The best assessment of Hugo's strange and lingering charm that I have read is by William Stafford, in *Crossing Unmarked Snow: Further Views on the Writer's Vocation*, edited by Paul Merchant and Vincent Wixon. In his essay "In Memoriam: Richard Hugo. 1923–1982," Stafford said of Hugo:

> In his breezy, risky way, he allowed what he said to lurch around and surprise people. . . . What was it that entranced this life for those who came to know it? Richard Hugo had learned how to savor loneliness, how to salvage lives and at the same time to celebrate failure and neglect. He put a tang of sweetness into the spectacle of sadness. Students could fail and succeed in an atmosphere of acceptance. A champion of slobs and losers, Hugo balanced pity and love while doing his own awkward dance of existence.
>
> To see him caring for his guests was to realize a new level of generosity. With what a wistful, piteous concern he peered into the refrig at night, fearful that the stores might close and leave the party lacking in ice cream.

For those of us who knew him, he will always remain haunting, a kind of cult figure. We need to feel we are welcome in the secret club we have formed.

The Poet as Clown

As TED KOOSER has pointed out, the convention of lyric poetry is such that, unless there are explicit indications to the contrary, the persona speaking a poem is a version of the author. Many of us who give poetry readings are conscious—painfully conscious—of how much easier it is to introduce a poem and tell of the occasion behind it than to actually read the poem. Watching and listening to the late Richard Hugo read—his introductions to his poems involved joking and storytelling and were often as rewarding as the poems themselves—I was struck by the similarities between a poetry reading and a stand-up comedy routine, and the similarity has not gone unnoticed. It is the basis of an excellent movie called *Punchline*, starring Tom Hanks, Sally Fields, and John Goodman.

The character Hanks plays is Steven Gold. Steven is from an upper-middle-class family, his father is a physician, and his parents expect him to become a doctor. He is enrolled in medical school, and he supports himself by moonlighting as a stand-up comedian in a small club called The Gas Station in lower Manhattan. As a comedian, he is gifted. As a medical student, he is not. It's not that he lacks the intelligence to study medicine. He lacks the interest. His natural bent is to turn everything into a joke. He is an artist.

In the movie's opening scene, we see another aspiring comedian, Lilah Krystick (played by Sally Fields) meeting a furtive-looking stranger in a seedy diner somewhere in lower Manhattan. He asks her if she has the money. She asks him if he has the jokes. He wants his money—twenty jokes at twenty-five dollars a pop: five hundred dollars. She demands to see one of them. He chides her: "No free samples." But he reaches into an envelope, draws out a card, and hands it to her. She reads aloud: "What does a Polish girl get that's long and hard when she gets married."

The scene shifts, and we watch Lilah performing her routine at The Gas Station. She bravely begins the Polish joke, but the punch line is supplied for her sarcastically by a member of the audience: "A last name." The jokes she was sold are worthless.

The movie cuts to Gold. He is being given an oral examination by a tribunal of three stone-faced doctors. Apparently he has made a suspiciously high score on an anatomy examination, and they believe that he must have had someone else take the test for him. With a pointer, they pick out specific organs on a colored chart displaying all the internal organs of a human body. He must supply the correct medical name of each. We watch him sweat. When the head examiner indicates one of the organs, Gold says, "The intestine?"

"What part of the intestine."

"The large intestine?"

"What part of the large intestine."

Gold asks coyly, "The poop chute?"

They are not amused. They rise as one and solemnly file down from the dais and out of the room, leaving him crushed and dazed. The head examiner pauses and grimly explains to Gold why he washed out. He concludes:

"What good does it do to have somebody with no talent for treating people with life-threatening illnesses?"

Gold replies with a joke: "It would cut down on the number of people with life-threatening illnesses?"

The examiner replies: "Is everything a joke to you?"

We begin to realize that Gold's joking is desperately serious.

Down in The Gas Station, where he is a rising star, he is under examination, too. A sort of jury of talent scouts is about to show up and observe him. On that night, his performance will be, in effect, an audition. If they like what they see, they can offer him a contract to appear on network television. Gold is the local star of the club, and we watch him improvising on the spot, by free association, like a jazz artist. He fabricates his humor from the darkest aspects of his personality. His humor is like Rodney Dangerfield's, delivered always at high pitch: half shout, half sob. One component of his humor is verbal. The other component is performance. It is this component that has traditionally distinguished stand-up comedy from poetry. Given the popularity of the live poetry reading and of the poetry slam, however, the distinction is less clear than it used to be.

The poetry reading is a comparatively recent phenomenon in the world of letters. For poets on the North Atlantic seaboard, it was almost certainly Dylan Thomas who popularized the oral reading of his own poems while on his American tours. But Thomas was regarded as a thrilling anomaly, a *poete maudit*, sui generis. It was Beat poetry, beginning in 1956 with Allen Ginsberg's famous reading in San Francisco's City Lights Bookstore of his poem "Howl," that launched in America the convention of the poetry reading and all its attendant paraphernalia. With the help of Lawrence Ferlinghetti and his publication of *A Coney Island of the Mind*, the live poetry reading became associated with jazz. A poetry reading was a kind of jam session.

In the oppressive context of fifties culture, the poetry reading was subversive, fun. And, indeed, the bantering between a poet and a live audience can be indistinguishable from stand-up comedy. The payoff for the poet is immediate. The introduction to a poem, when the poet reveals to the audience the occasion of the poem, is apt to give both the poet and the audience far more immediate pleasure than the reading of the poem itself. Indeed, in the poetry of many contemporaries—Galway Kinnell and Robert Bly come to mind—we find poets who have cultivated a style specially suited for public reading. Poems in this style don't require study beforehand. Like jokes, they function as one-shot deals; for the performance potential of a poem and its silent-reading potential are almost mutually exclusive. Only a very few poets—such as Yeats—wrote poems that performed as well as they read. Today, however, the poet is expecting, hoping to be thronged with fans after a reading, like a rock music star. And, indeed, it was in the late fifties when Louis Simpson coined the term *Po-Biz* to describe the poetry world.

Coincidentally (though perhaps it was no coincidence), just around the time when Beat poetry popularized the poetry reading, Elvis Presley overturned conventional popular music. Pat Boone–like crooning was replaced by an adversarial music. Just as the year 1913 marks the invention of a free-verse, adversarial poetry now known as "modernist"—a poetry that would replace conventional, somewhat sentimental rhyming, accentual-syllabic poetry—so did the year 1957, with the appearance of Presley on the *Ed Sullivan Show*, mark the beginning of the revolution that was the beginning of rock music, overturning the sentimental status quo. Because rock music was more compelling to the young than poetry was, it captured most of the youth culture, who would now prefer a Bruce Springsteen concert to a poetry reading. The subculture of the poetry reading was suddenly and sharply delimited. It was no longer popular. It was highbrow, which is to say that its venue became the university.

Most American poetry is solemn. Its main topic might be called the Topic of Desire (often sexual). Other topics are conventionally handled by other genres. But humor in American poetry is comparatively rare. Whitman, in *Song of Myself*, is occasionally uproarious, but the best American humor in literature is, like Mark Twain's, in prose. What about contemporary poets? I can count the successful American humorists on the fingers of one hand. Who are they? The reigning king and prince of humor are Paul Zimmer and William Trowbridge respectively. Other poets who display humor frequently and with success are Jack Myers, Roger Weingarten, Mark Halliday, William Kloefkorn, R. S. Gwynn, and Richard Moore.

Humor in American poetry has been written about definitively by

Ronald Wallace in *God Be with the Clown* (Missouri, 1984). In the introduction to that book, Wallace distinguishes between two traditional comic archetypes: "the *alazon* [epitomized by Whitman] who claims to know more than he does . . . an *eiron* [epitomized by Dickinson] who pretends ignorance, seeming to know less than he [she] does." Perhaps the most predictable feature of humorous poetry in America is its conspicuous deployment of a persona—of the author as a character. In the poems of Paul Zimmer, this character is named "Zimmer." As Jan Susina writes in the introduction to his book *Poet as Zimmer, Zimmer as Poet*:

> Reading the poetry of Paul Zimmer, one might recall Yeats's remark that before sitting down to write, the poet must first conceive the poetic self that he wishes to display in his poems.
>
> While the most obvious organizational device in the poetry of Paul Zimmer is the set of personal references centering around a remarkable fellow named Zimmer, Paul Zimmer is not so much a confessional poet in the manner of Lowell . . . but a skillful manipulator of the persona like Yeats or Browning. . . . Whether speaking in the voice of Zimmer or Wanda or any other of the memorable characters who appear and reappear with regularity within the poems, his is a voice . . . with a fine sense of the absurdity and ironies of life which frequently lead us to sad wisdom.

To test the truth of Susina's analysis, let us look at a poem by Zimmer:

Zimmer Envying Elephants

I have a wide, friendly face
Like theirs, yet I can't hang
My nose like a fractured arm
Nor flap my dishpan ears.
I can't curl my canine teeth,
Swing my tail like a filthy tassel,
Nor make thunder without lightning.

But I'd like to thud amply around
For a hundred years or more,
Stuffing an occasional tree top

Into my mouth, screwing hugely for
Hours at a time, gaining weight,
And slowly growing a few hairs.

Once in a while I'd charge a power pole
Or smash a wall down just to keep
Everybody loose and at a distance.

Though as I have already remarked, the performance potential of a poem
and its potential as a silent reading experience are generally incommensurable, this poem has both. Its performance potential, however, is greater
than its silent-reading potential, as I can attest, having watched Zimmer
read this poem to a live audience.

The presence of a live audience adds an intangible ingredient to
poetry. It can paralyze the poet with anxiety; it can encourage the poet too
much, so that the poet will go on and on, as if totally unaware, after an
hour and ten minutes, that the audience can barely restrain itself from
leaving. But if the poetry has a joke-like character, the presence of an
audience is essential to maximize the poem's potential. In G. Legman's
The Rationale of the Dirty Joke, Legman points out the public nature of jokes:

> Under the mask of humor, our society allows infinite aggressions by
> everyone and against everyone. In the culminating laugh by the lis-
> tener or observer—whose position is often really that of the victim
> or butt—the teller of the joke betrays his hidden hostility and signals
> his victory by being, theoretically at least, the one person who does
> not laugh . . . The listener's expected laughter is, therefore . . . a shriv-
> ing of the teller, a reassurance that he has not been caught.

In Legman's terms, "Zimmer Envying Elephants," when read before a
live audience, is a means by which Zimmer can blame the audience for
possibly patronizing him for his frumpy build or for countless other
injuries which they (the epitome of "normal" people) may have inflicted
on him at *any* time: for ignoring him as a child, for teasing him in high
school, for not regarding him as the sensitive special fellow that he is and
that most people are in their own eyes. The last stanza is a threat of what
he would like to do to them.

Recently, I was reading in the *New Yorker Magazine* an essay about the comedy of Albert Brooks. The only time the essay took on light was when it rendered the wheedling intensity of Brooks's comic delivery:

> "All I do for a living is to be exposed. That's all I am. I'm *exposed*. So if I didn't have the one little area that's not exposed, a few inches, I'd go nuts. I can tolerate if a person thinks I'm fat or thin or ugly. I can read that in the newspapers and be O.K. . . . But once, a long time ago, I let somebody into a house, and they wrote about—They didn't like— The room looked *dark* to them. *That* bothered me. My house isn't onstage. I am."

The monologue above captures pretty accurately Brooks's dialect, especially toward the end where he comes down hard on certain words. But unless the reader has actually *heard* Brooks, the reader will interpolate Brooks's personality incompletely from the printed script .

Because performance art is so difficult to render on the printed page, without an actual videotape the best a commentator can do for a reading audience is try to describe the physical appearance and the body language of a performer, asking the reader to imagine the physical venue of the performance.

The best comic performer I've ever heard on the poetry circuit is William Trowbridge, performing his King Kong poems. The title poem of Trowbridge's book *Enter Dark Stranger* tells the audience where Trowbridge is coming from:

> In *Shane*, when Palance first appears,
> a stray cur takes one look and slinks away
> on tiptoes, able, we understand, to recognize
> something truly dark. So it seems
> when we appear, crunching through the woods.
> A robin cocks his head, then hops off,
> ready to fly like hell and leave us the worm.
> . . .

The alarm spreads in a skittering
of squirrels, finches, millipedes. Imagine
a snail picking up the hems of his shell
and hauling ass for cover. He's studied carnivores,
seen the menu, noticed the escargots.

But forget Palance, who would have murdered Alabama
just for fun. Think of Karloff's monster,

This is excellent poetry, but to appreciate the full effect of the wit, you
have to be facing Trowbridge, with his balding head, his suspenders, and
hear his casual, drawling, offhand style of delivery, as if Mark Twain were
in the room, sparkling with a malice delivered so gently it looked at first
ingratiating.

The poem that immediately follows "Enter," "Kong Looks Back on
His Tryout with the Bears"—the first of twelve "Kong" poems—is nar-
rated by Kong himself:

If it had worked out, I'd be on a train to Green Bay,
not crawling up this building with the air corps
on my ass. And if it weren't for love, I'd drop
this shrieking little bimbo sixty stories
and let them take me back to the exhibit,
let them teach me to rhumba and do imitations.
They tried me on the offensive line, told me
to take out the right cornerback for Nagurski.
Eager to please, I wadded up the whole secondary,
then stomped the line, then the bench and locker room,
then the east end of town, to the river.
But they were not pleased: they said
I had to learn my position, become a team player.
. . .
So I was put on waivers right after camp,
and here I am, panty sniffer, about to die a clown,
who once opened a hole you could drive Nebraska through.

As with any good joke, the entire poem exists in order to deliver its punch
line (in this case the poem's last two lines). The poem is a good one on
the page. But performed, it's even better. Watching Trowbridge perform

these Kong poems, I thought that he was as good a stand-up comic as I had ever heard.

I felt similarly when hearing William Kloefkorn read at Emporia State. Kloefkorn's persona is that of a wise, tough-minded old farmer who has seen everything and who, underneath his realism, entertains a fierce, mischievous, bawdy streak, a crotchety defiance. As Northrop Frye writes in *The Anatomy of Criticism*:

> The satirist may employ a plain, common-sense, conventional person as a foil for the various *alazons* of society. Such a person may be the author himself or a narrator, and he corresponds to the plain dealer in comedy . . . When distinguished from the author, he is often a rustic with pastoral affinities . . . The kind of American satire that passes as folk humor, exemplified by . . . Artemus Ward and Will Rogers, makes a good deal of him.

Here is an example of Kloefkorn's satire:

Eating Prime Rib
Shortly After Being Advised
To Stay The Hell Away From All Red Meat

I am eating the bad news
my friend has washed his hands of,
that immortal friend

who lives by feeding
on the decline of others,
that humorless theologian

whose text at my funeral
will come from the Book of Spite:
I told you so—

that same text
another preacher will use
when my own preacher's form of redness

nails him,
that everlasting tongue
getting the last wag in.

It's an old story, this flesh,
an ancient myth that needs
to be put down from time to time

to keep it sweet
if not quite plausible,
its message lying in that brief silence

between the heavings
of *Sturm and Drang.* So
count on it,

in the morning a cardinal
red as blood
cutting into your dream,

the body rising from its heavy bed
thankful
for all that grace

it yet has time to snub
before too late, or maybe not,
it learns.

A fine, fierce poem reminiscent of Stevens's "A High-Toned Old Christian Woman," Kloefkorn's poem satirizes every form of piety.

The closest to being a stand-up comedian a poet comes is when, like Steven Gold in *Punchline,* he is speaking directly to the audience about his own feelings, when his persona, like that of "Zimmer," is himself—for example Jack Myers in his poem "Headache":

I tried to remember to buy aspirin and soap
but I only bought the aspirin.
I liked the way that worked, the way I made my choice
unbeknownst to me. It was clean, as if I knew something
way down deep.

Because what if I only bought the soap?
Then I'd be locked out of my head in pain

trying to reach my brain by transcendental meditation,
which only makes the pain more real.

On the other hand, what if I bought both,
which may be normal:
what if I remembered everything?

No thanks, I want to know who's on first.
I want my mind made up even if it means
I don't feel normal, or I have to keep a list,
which reminds me

of my delivery bike which George Lynch stole
and then he sold it and I got fired and then
he moved away. He is no more to me
than the window of light shining on that apple seed.
Besides, I'd rather be right than clean,
the little prick.

"I want my mind made up even if it means / I don't feel normal." "I
don't feel normal" is reminiscent of Robert Lowell's line in "Skunk Hour,"
"my mind's not right," describing Lowell's presentiment of a manic
descent, except that, unlike the muttered Lowell line, Myers's is reassuring: he can laugh at himself and invite us to admit, in an almost com-
munal setting, our own foibles. The poem is a lot like Blake's famous,
wise little poem "A Poison Tree":

I was angry with my friend:
I told my wrath, my wrath did end.
I was angry with my foe:
I told it not, my wrath did grow.

And I watered it in fears,
Night & morning with my tears;
. . .
And it grew both day and night
Till it bore an apple bright;
And my foe beheld its shine,
And he knew that it was mine,

Like Blake, Myers is quite aware not only of the deliberate nature of his spite but also of the result of gunnysacking his grievance. When we reach the last line, with its release of pent-up anger, we realize that the entire poem is about gunnysacking, regarding such behavior with an amusement that is ironic, sad, yet wickedly complicit: it was fun to say "the little prick." In his exaggerated self-consciousness and in his consciousness of self-consciousness, Myers has been juggling several balls at once. He is parodying Sartrean existentialism and the solemnity of philosophical introspection in general. He has been mocking the Cartesian premise "I think therefore I am" by applying it to apparent trivia. In this respect, Myers's poem, with its desperate wisecracking, reminds me of the comedy of Woody Allen. Indeed, Myers may be the contemporary Woody Allen of our poets.

In terms of Northrop Frye's *Anatomy*, the mode of the stand-up comic is preeminently the Mythos of Winter, and it is a mode particularly suited to television. As the "Comment" pages of the July 11, 1994, issue of the *New Yorker* observed:

> Exactly thirty years ago, when Marshall McLuhan envisioned the global village—the place, at which we have now arrived, of everybody's instant access to everything—he assumed, optimistically, that it would produce a world of instant understanding, in which we would all be neighbors and what each of us was doing would be known to all the rest of us. Nobody could have foreseen that life in the global village was actually going to be like life in a village.

The "global village" envisioned by McLuhan would be characterized by an "oral, tribal" culture, and he was right. It's a world of gossip. To watch the *Jay Leno Show* is to catch up on the day's events and see them converted into brilliant, bitter jokes about contemporary figures who, in five years, few people will remember: Tanya Harding, Gennifer Flowers. But who in the reading audience now remembers the infamous English call girl Christine Keeler in the Profumo spy scandal?

Everything, in the domain of "current events," is topical, and television has returned us to a culture analogous to the high Augustan culture of Pope and Swift, "Augustan" with an American spin. Like Twain's humor, or Trowbridge's or Kloefkorn's or Myers's, our stand-up comedy is democratic and profoundly populist. It can smell shit and pretentiousness from miles away. It feels free to say so.

William Stafford

Genius in Camouflage

In 1972, five years before driving to Missoula, Montana, to interview Richard Hugo, I was a student in the Ph.D. program at the University of Colorado. I was driving into Denver with my friend Reg Saner to conduct a Poets-in-the-Schools program. We had turned off U.S. 36 onto I-25 and were heading straight toward downtown Denver when, in one of those moments James Hillman discusses in *The Soul's Code*, dictated, perhaps, by one's daemon, I realized what I should do with my studies— with my life. I should drop the pathetic idea of doing a thesis in medieval literature to please some father figure and instead do a thesis in twentieth-century American literature, about William Stafford. My thesis would be immediately publishable, for there were no books about him. Best of all, I could drive out to Lake Oswego and interview him for the book. I could actually meet him.

The first time I met him was in July 1972 at his house. He was fifty-eight. It was thrilling to meet him, but it was daunting, too, because he was so much like my own father, Alan. Wirey, elfin, with the face of a fox, Stafford was curious about everything around him, absolutely alert. Alan had graduated from Harvard with a B.S. in chemistry in 1925, the year after Stanley Kunitz had. They both graduated summa cum laude. All my life I had been surrounded by Bell Labs physicists gossiping about who was in line for the Nobel Prize this year, who was at Cal Tech, who was at Cambridge at the Cavendish Laboratory, who was at M.I.T. (The gossip of scientists is depressingly similar to the gossip of writers.) Like the Bell

Labs scientists, Bill was on the leading edge of his field, lecturing every-where, everywhere in demand. He was a genius. From being in the presence of Bell Labs geniuses for my entire childhood, I'd learned to recognize them, like a bird-watcher. I had to. It was a kind of survival technique, to avoid making a fool of oneself in the presence of some of the most high-powered intellectuals in the world. Some of them had worked with J. Robert Oppenheimer on the Manhattan Project. Los Alamos had been their vortex.

In his book *Alone with America*, Richard Howard refers to the "arrogant otherness" of the persona in Stafford's first poetry collection, *West of Your City*. It has been pointed out by the poet/critic Judith Kitchen that "West of Your City" alludes to Frost's title *North of Boston*. "Your city" is Boston. "You" is Frost. Howard, the quintessential New Yorker and European traveler, is right, but only partially. Stafford's "otherness" wasn't arrogant. It was the otherness of every major mind I've had the privilege to observe. It was the neutral, appraising, canny posture of intellectuality—an appetite that is aesthetic, amoral, and endlessly curious. And cold. What must have it been like having Stafford as a father? Not easy. It is now legendary how Stafford, so as not to disturb his family, would get up well before dawn to write. He described the routine in his poem "Mornings":

> Quiet,
> rested, the brain begins to burn
> and glow like a coal in the dark,
> early—four in the morning, cold, with
> frost on the lawn.

We are familiar, too, with Stafford's cooperative venture with his son Kim: the book *Braided Apart*. We are less familiar with the fact that Stafford's eldest son, Brett, killed himself. Brett must have felt as I did: compared to Alan, I would never measure up. Virtually Alan's last words to me—we were discussing Wittgenstein—were, "Son, until you know German, you'll never understand Western culture."

When Stafford's son Kim visited Kansas State in the fall of 1998, as the primary speaker in a conference in honor of William Stafford, he and

I talked about Brett's suicide in 1988. Kim said that the suicide had been about a love affair and that his father had said of Brett: "He wasn't mean enough."

Meanwhile, the mistaken identification of Stafford as a "regional" poet continues: In the New York Times obituary of August 31, 1993, the headline read, "William Edgar Stafford, Professor and Poet of the West, Dies at 79." The writer, Wolfgang Saxon, wrote:

> Both his life and his writing looked westward or to the Northwest, and he found his themes in small-town family life and in nature. His work was infused with the vast expanses of desert and prairie, mountain ranges and sky.

Like a fox, like a wildcat, Stafford lived his life in camouflage. He camouflaged his true nature. A poem which for me epitomizes this camouflage is his poem "For the Governor" in Someday, Maybe:

For the Governor

Heartbeat by heartbeat our governor tours
the state, and before a word and after a word
over the crowd the world speaks to him,
thin as a wire. And he knows inside
each word, too, that anyone says,
another word lurks, and inside that . . .

Sometimes we fear for him: he, or someone,
must act for us all. Across our space
we watch him while the country leans
on him: he bears time's tall demand,
and beyond our state he must think the shore
and beyond that the waves and the miles and
        the waves.

On the surface, the poem is about a man campaigning for the governorship of a state like Kansas. But read closely, the poem yields a second meaning. The poem is about the relation of the mind to the body. "Across our space / we watch him while the country leans / on him: he bears time's tall demand." The mind is able to conceive of its end, the body's eventual death. Moreover, the mind is able to conceive of itself: consciousness of consciousness is what makes us particularly human. This, the poem's true issue—Stafford's intellectuality—has been camouflaged. I asked him about a female figure named Ella who appears in some of his poems about rural Kansas life. He remarked that "Ella" is a female third-person pronoun.

A second well-known poem, "Report from a Far Place," camouflages its sophistication in a way that is also typically Staffordian. The poem reads:

Making these word things to
step on across the world, I
could call them snowshoes.

They creak, sag, bend, but
hold, over the great deep cold,
and they turn up at the toes.

In war or city or camp
they could save your life;
you can muse them by the fire.

Be careful though: they
burn, or don't burn, in their own
strange way, when you say them.

At first glance, this poem appears to be about writing, "making word things." Read closely, however, it appears to be more about reading than about writing, especially the lines "In war or city or camp / they could save your life; / you can muse them by the fire." The cleverest line, though, is the offhanded remark "and they turn up at the toes." Often, in Stafford poems, casual asides are profound. If we think of the way in which the turned-up toes of skis or snowshoes deflect the snow, deflect the world, we find a metaphor for the way in which the abstract nature of words deflects the world from us and thus keeps us from suffocating in existence, allowing us to ride "on top of" things momentarily. The title puzzles us, until we remember that in Stafford's symbolic vocabulary "near" means "kindred" and "far" means "different." The "far" place which imposes "word things" upon the world is the mind.

There is another side of Stafford, though, that dispenses with camouflage. It is not affable. It is fierce. We glimpse this side, at the end of "Our City Is Guarded by Automatic Rockets," where he says:

> There is a place behind our hill so real
> it makes me turn my head, no matter. There
> in the last thicket lies the cornered cat
> saved by its claws, now ready to spend
> all that is left of the wilderness, embracing
> its blood. And that is the way I will spit
> life, at the end of any trail where I smell any hunter.

The last piece Stafford published before his death was a review of the anthology *Against Forgetting: Twentieth-Century Poetry of Witness*, edited by Carolyn Forche. His approach to the anthology is prickly:

> But there are inherent problems in a collection like this. For instance, the individual glimpses that create the distinction of poetry put a strain on the thesis of the book; books that buckle down to the thesis can hardly attain the shiver of the unexpected that distinguishes lively discourse. We can be informed; we can encounter the thoughts and emotions of significant people . . . but it takes something more to validate the poetry experience.

And later in the review he writes:

> A further problem above achieving authenticity in a survey like this one lurks everywhere in the selections: quality is primary, but the need for wide representation put a strain on that criterion. And how vividly do you have to suffer in order to qualify? . . .
>
> I feel a bump when the explanatory text says, "The Germans decided." All Germans? And similarly when Carolyn Forche says, "My new work seemed controversial to my American contemporaries." (Who, me?) The labels in the book . . . put a torque on me, snagged my attention, kept me wary of living on the emotional high of atrocity hunger.

Morally and intellectually exacting as Stafford's mind was, there was a softer side to him. I glimpsed it most vividly in the summer of 1987, when he and I were on the staff of the Port Townsend Writers Conference. Several of us were being driven back to Fort Worden State Park from dinner at a restaurant. Stafford was in the front seat. Marvin Bell was beside me in the middle seat. As we drove past a brightly lit bar that was the students' hangout, Marvin called to the driver to let him out there. Stafford burst out to Marvin: "Must you?" It was a motherly gesture, pure reflex, like a mother instinctively reaching out to stop a toddler from walking into a busy street. I realized that he loved Marvin.

When, the day after Stafford suffered his heart attack at home, Henry Taylor called me with the news, my first thought was, "How lucky to go like that, that cleanly," and that Stafford had indeed led a lucky life. He himself had told me as much, years ago at Stephens College, when I had invited him there. I don't remember what I was mumbling to him, but he suddenly faced me and glared at me, pure wildcat: "You don't understand." He hissed it. "I was just lucky." He took nothing for granted. And I thought, also, of Willa Cather's famous story "Neighbor Rosicky":

> The old farmer looked up at the doctor with a gleam of amusement in his queer, triangular-shaped eyes. . . . Rosicky's face had the habit of looking interested—suggested a contented disposition and a reflective quality that was gay rather than grave. This gave him a certain detachment, the easy manner of an onlooker and observer.

The end of the story describes Rosicky's friendship with his daughter-in-law, Polly:

> She had a sudden feeling that nobody in the world, not her mother, not Rudolph, or anyone really loved her as much as old Rosicky did. It perplexed her. She sat frowning and trying to puzzle it out. It was as if Rosicky had a special gift for loving people, something that was like an ear for music or an eye for colour. It was quiet, unobtrusive; it was merely there. . . . After he dropped off to sleep, she sat holding his warm, broad, flexible brown hand. She had never seen another in the least like it. She wondered if it wasn't a kind of gipsy hand, it was so alive and quick and light in its communications—very strange in

a farmer. Nearly all of the farmers she knew had huge lumps of fists, like mauls, or they were knotty and bony and uncomfortable looking, with stiff fingers. But Rosicky's hand was like quicksilver, flexible, muscular, . . . it was a warm brown hand, with some cleverness in it, . . . and something else which Polly could only call "gipsy-like" —something nimble and lively and sure, in the way that animals are.

I would like to imagine that William Stafford died as Rosicky did, as described by Willa Cather:

> After he had taken a few stitches, the cramp began in his chest, like yesterday. He put his pipe down cautiously on the window-sill and bent over to ease the pull. No use—he had better try to get to bed if he could. He rose and groped his way across the familiar floor, which was rising and falling like the deck of a ship. At the door he fell. When Mary came in, she found him lying there, and the moment she touched him she knew that he was gone.

In my experience, Cather is the only author to describe accurately, without sentimentality, in the figure of Rosicky, the mysterious, inexplicable quality of human goodness—its elusiveness, its disinterestedness, its absence of vanity. William Stafford understood all this. He lived it. Determined to keep the truth of his genius from embarrassing us, he camouflaged it as carefully, as considerately as he could.

Meanwhile, in this "half-savage country" that is America, the position of poetry will always be as marginal and as generally misunderstood as higher mathematics, as Beethoven's last string quartets, or as Stafford's choosing to be a C.O. in 1942 during World War II—as distrusted as intellectuality itself. Probably the most exacting account of this that I have ever found is the preface to Mary Kinzie's book *The Judge Is Fury.*

The Judge Is Fury

The Moral Urgency of
Mary Kinzie's Ghost Ship

In her preface to her collection of poetry reviews, *The Judge Is Fury*, the poet/critic Mary Kinzie presents the following parable:

> A man wakens in a desert with a continuous thong, like a Mobius strip, drawn so cleverly about his ankles that he can neither untie it nor walk upright. He stands, falls, stands, starts to hobble, falls, stands again. He does brief, birdlike leaps, one foot slightly behind the other. He becomes better at this. He drinks from muddy pools; he eats roots. Having nothing to do in this wasteland with its monotonous horizon, he becomes adept at long leaps upward, then forward; he practices coming down so as to raise only the lightest puff of dust from the friable earth. A whimsical interpolation of this allegory would have us believe that a circus travels past the man and seeing his graceful movements engages him to be its rope dancer high above the audience. What is beyond dispute is that the moment someone cut the thong it was as if the Achilles tendons had been severed and the man could neither dance nor walk. . . .
>
> If it be asked whether one couldn't have learned to rope-dance anyway, the answer would have to be, How could one stop striding ahead for long enough to stumble back upon the alien measures of rope-dancing? To be an apprentice is to learn someone else's angle of vision till one is blind with it. Like writing with the wrong hand, learning art is at first as unnatural as any broken habit. Over time, this thwarting and unpleasant wrongness is absorbed and adjusted until it not only casts no shadow but even enables one's very seeing, dexterity, and repose.

This amazing passage is the equal, in my mind, to the best parables of Franz Kafka: haunting and, regarding the motive and the placement of the art of poetry in contemporary America, absolutely accurate. Kinzie then recalls J. V. Cunningham's mordant quatrain with its unnerving clause casting all the neatly fitting poetic relationships into doubt:

> These the assizes: here the charge, denial,
> Proof and disproof: the poem is the trial.
> Experience is defendant, and the jury
> Peers of tradition, and the judge is fury.

She concludes:

> The present age is not (if any age was ever) propitious for poetry . . . .
> But then, mercifully, from time to time, when there is some conver-
> sation with the past, some familiarity with forms, some breadth of
> human interests, and some flexible familiarity with fury, the cruel
> hobble one was given, one relaxes. Not into mediocrity but into a
> kind of hurricane's eye.

A similar view of art was promulgated over fifty years earlier by T. S. Eliot in the essay "Tradition and the Individual Talent"—a *similar* view but nowise an identical one. As we know now, the poet's personal life in Eliot's poetry was disguised. Indeed, the best approach to Eliot's poetry is to treat him as a playwright—a dramatist—rather than a lyric poet. In only one poem, "Ash Wednesday," does he approach explicit autobiogra-phy. His other poems are artful disguises—a Jamesean character (not unlike John Marcher) in "The Love Song of J. Alfred Prufock"; Tiresias and a cast of other characters in *The Waste Land*; a late Beethoven string quartet (Opus 132, in A-minor); and, perhaps, Stephane Mallarme in *Four Quartets*. The nature of Eliot's actual character we can only infer, and many of the details, particularly his treatment of his first wife, Vivien Haigh Wood, do not speak well for him. As he wrote:

> It is not in his personal emotions, the emotions provoked by particu-
> lar events in his life, that the poet is in any way remarkable or inter-
> esting. His particular emotions may be simple, or crude, or flat . . .
> Consequently, we must believe that "emotion recollected in tranquil-

ity" is an inexact formula . . . . Poetry is not a turning loose of emotion, but an escape from personality; it is not the expression of personality, but an escape from personality. But, of course, only those who have personality and emotions know what it means to want to escape from these things.

Mary Kinzie, like all of the best postmodern poets, does not use disguises; but she is a formalist at heart. It is significant, I think, that Kinzie begins each of her lines with a capital letter, and the diversity of forms in her latest poetry collection, Ghost Ship, is extravagant, ranging from the long-lined free verse of "Cilantro" to elegant, end-rhymed lyrics like "Clover Cross":

> Below my hand what do I see
> As I comb through the grass?
> A moon of light on each shamrock
> That sharpens as I pass. . . ?

The forms do not constrain Kinzie, they liberate her. Her poems validate once again Richard Wilbur's famous analogy of form as a necessary bottle in which to house the genie of content, feeling. A case in point would be the poem "Early December," a sestina containing echoes of Amy Lowell's famous "Patterns." Here, Kinzie describes longing for her partner. The poem begins:

> Everything seems sad, even this writing.
> The ground is dark. Why won't it start snowing?
> That would be something—like a long white letter
> Through the black mailbox's grillwork pattern
> Come to my address across some distance
> Subtle with the question mark of volume.
>
> The air around me is a closing volume:
> Tasks I should be at instead of writing,
> Poetry postpones into the distance—

At the close of the sestina comes the envoy, beginning "I miss your body. Still, snowing makes the distance / Into patterns." The envoy is plaintive and unusually long—nine lines with their end-rhymes, ECA, ECA, ECA, like a distress signal, a phone left off the hook. The only other "mid-career" formalist I know of who can do this as well as Kinzie does it is Marilyn Hacker. Well, almost as well.

This book has vision, and much of it is contained in its title poem, a kind of ode addressed to Kinzie's daughter, who in the poem is six years old. A significant poem with which to compare this poem might be Sharon Olds's "Language of the Brag," which is quoted in my chapter on "Rhetoricity." The ethos of Kinzie's author/persona speaking "Ghost Ship" is more credible than Olds's. Kinzie is not out to shock the reader in the somewhat mechanical way that Olds is. Kinzie begins:

> A mother's love—my love for you—hurts at the core
> Like a coal whitened by long burning,
> Nothing of me unsinged by your existence. Odd,
> How the metaphors of love grow dangerous: You pour
> Out of perfection death in all its low
> Centrifugal furor—essentially, the flame
> Of consciousness, which flickers around the life
> That life begins to eat.

We are back to the existential issue that haunts so much postmodern poetry—consciousness of consciousness. But Kinzie's poem differs from the typical postmodern poem of ontology. It embodies a convincing and heartfelt ethos. Kinzie worries about the world into which she has fostered a child. She has discovered how having a child tethers one umbilically to the world, to the future.

In the most uncompromisingly searching passage in the poem, Kinzie describes buying her daughter flowers in a "run-down retail greenhouse" and, because of the lower-class appearance of the woman selling them, warning her daughter not to touch anything. Kinzie's view of "pity" and of her own comfortable life is as merciless as Blake's:

> A pretty view, in well connected words
> That hint how genial is pity for
> These charcoal sketches of a helpless wasting.
> False work by easy virtue, making views.

What could be truer? What if it were here
In the run-down retail greenhouse.
Where I brought you to buy flowers, to plant
Like sparkling knots of water near the hedges,
—What if this were the naval of disease?
Irrigation runnels of concrete
Broken against a mossy mould that stank
Of cats and urine . . . The long house of glass
Squinting along the trays of half-dead seedlings
Among which humped the manic, injured cat . . .
At last a woman, teeth stained, filthy hands,
Hot pants on her soft, attractive thighs,
An orange dye hanging on her hair,
Slurring of the eyes and tongue, would serve us
Where she stood in reeking light. I snarled,
"Stay right behind me," and this frightened you.
Even when this pitiful, used creature
Offered you out of her patchwork heart
Some mangy flowers, I hissed, "Don't touch a thing."
—Is this where it begins? Not just disease
But worse, the complications of recoil
That drive the blood up with self-satisfaction?
How can we save you then?
                                        Even the wish
Unworthy, given all those dead. I know this.

What else to say? Like many of the poems in *Ghost Ship*, this one is Shake-
spearean in its lavishness, its harvesting of echoes going back to the
Garden. This is what became of Eve. This is what could become of any
daughter. This is knowledge. It shows the author/persona to be upper-
middle class and prejudiced. But it shows also her knowingness about it
and her guilt about it.

It is a courageous poem.

Divine Honors

Hilda Raz and the Music of Pain

Divine Honors is best summarized in the blurbs on the back cover by Walter McDonald and Marilyn Hacker. McDonald writes: "In Divine Honors, we're in for a head-on collision with grief, the inescapable fact of cancer." Hacker's blurb suggests immediately the book's significant epistemological issues, ones that transcend the book's story and are about how to deal, in language, not just with soul pain but with physical pain.

> Transgressive and transcendent, Hilda Raz's new poems are intimately involved with the physical, corporeal world, and constantly making the leap of faith necessary for its re-embodiment in words. These poems push the boundaries of what language can do to enunciate perception.

The collection is in five sections, framed by a prologue and an afterword, and it is a narrative of the events, beginning in 1988, when Raz was diagnosed with breast cancer and had one breast removed. The narration recalls the confessional poems of Sexton, Plath, Snodgrass, and Hugo, but it transcends self-display and self-pity. It is, among many things, a tough-minded accounting of womanhood and aging. The poems are "lyric" in the purest sense of the word. They are highly conscious of music. They view music as a source of spiritual definition, and they are intended to be sung—not necessarily out loud but as a kind of (probably secular) prayer. The importance of music is suggested by a poem in the prologue, "Isaac Stern's Performance":

Here plants—gold and dry—rustle up
green at soil's edge.
Music roils the room
where I wait, my chest holding even
at the scar's edge.

Whatever chances I took
paid off and now I have only
the rest of my life to consider.
Once it was a globe, an ocean
to cross, at least a desert—
now a rivulet, or a blowhole.

"I remember it was like a story,"
Rampal said on the radio.
"He told you the Beethoven concerto."
I am telling you cancer.

I am telling you like moisture
at soil's edge after winter, or
the bulb of the amaryllis you brought
raising stem after stem from cork dirt,
one hybrid flower after another unfurling
for hours, each copper petal opening its throat so
slowly, each shudder of tone—mahogany, coral, blood—
an ache, orgasm, agony, life.

"You," the muse of this collection, later appears as Raz's "daughter,"
Sarah. But "you" also refers to the long scar left by the mastectomy.

The main metaphors of this collection involve gardening and the
discoveries which her involvement with earth (and Earth) lead Raz toward
in the context of cancer. Music as a necessary and inevitable expression
of the inner life is the second main theme, though so deeply is it impli-
cated with the book's vision that this may not be immediately apparent.
The ground of this "music" is presented in the book's last poem, "Vowels,"
before the epilogue:

Holes on the page
the eye picks up,
the ear opens to,
the I finds irresistible.

Wide mouth bass
drift on weeds
by the dam's breach.
A lake
in upper New York state,
a pond near Syracuse,
both yield their fish
to the lone fisherman
in autumn, his monofilament line
hissing and dripping over water.
"Watch the bowl the line makes . . ."
He touches her breast with his ear
as she cradles him now, against
an oval to break his heart
so she moans, or he does
touching her here . . .
So they begot music
and were saved.
And the ewe was in the thicket
well used, and the fish ground
in the mortar, and the horseradish
and another year
turned.

The vowel being explored here is the long-*o* sound, with all of its connotations: wonder, pain, desire, terror—and, of course, zero. Here, Raz
achieves what Gertrude Stein projects in the epigraph to part 3: *Was there
not a way of naming things that would not invent names, but mean names without naming
them?*

The other sound Raz explores is far more primal than long o, and
lodged at the heart of this book's best poem, a poem which is surely
equal to the poems of the great Russian poet Anna Akhmatova:

Mu

. . . the old root giving rise to mystery was mu, with cognates MYSTICAL and MUTE. MYSTERY came from the Greek muein with the meaning of closing the lips, closing the eyes.

—Lewis Thomas

Misery a block in the head
a block I hum mmmm through, the way mother
mmmm helps me move to. Umber attaches to shadows
in hedge-ribbons. Feet mmmmmmmm, hit-sounds like murder
stitched to lips, the miles, hummm, eyes shut shuttered, cement
    walk
studded with dark I'm afraid mmmmmo
and now I am come alone at midnight onto the pineneedles of
    the park.

I am come to say good-bye in the dark but my mouth won't open.
What opens is my eye to the open edge of the metal tunnel under
the curve of the spiral slide I'm afraid to rise to. I'm standing at the
base to cry out at midnight Whose children will come down? Who
bashes into my arms so we open our mou ths to this cadence no no
no no mmm mommy up again to ride the big slide they and I
    falling
into the dark air. Open is the mouth of the metal tunnel.
Tomorrow, mmmmu, the knife.

In the very middle of this collection we come to its other most crucial
poem, "Petting the Scar," dedicated to Alicia Ostriker. Its tone is feisty.

You know what? I don't want a brave death,
faithful children mopping up after my body,
sweet thing, nubbly fissures and skin so soft
it's silklike. . . .
You tell me to reach under my shirt and pet the scar.
. . .
Under my robe—I must put down my pen to do it—
my palm feels chill: this is not a metaphor
but an image, true, a fact: I swear it.

No pouty lip the color of eyelids. A cold blank.
But the scar!
Riverroad, meandering root, stretched coil, wire chord, embroidery
    in its loop, mine, my body.

Oh, love!

I guess I have to quit, but there is still entirely too much to say about
this collection. Wasn't it Lewis Thomas who maintained that a species
which contained the music of Johann Sebastian Bach couldn't be totally
hopeless? Divine Honors is, in my opinion, a book that will end being, like
Plath's Ariel, a classic, but for the right reasons: for the character, for the
courage, for the sheer power of mind, and for the consummate artistry
of Hilda Raz.

Conclusion

In the April 1997 issue of *Harpers* there is reprinted the keynote address given by Richard Howard in May 1996 at the PEN Literary Awards ceremony in New York City. Howard described the various ways in which poetry has been "commodified" and then offered a prescription for saving it.

> If we are to save poetry, which means if we are to savor it, we must restore poetry to that status of seclusion and even secrecy which characterizes only our authentic pleasures and identifies only our intimately valued actions. . . . Poetry will flourish—in terminal capitalism as in terminating communism—only when it is harder to find, when it is perceived as a valuable and virtually disallowed production that must be sought by need and by desire. We must eroticize the situation of poetry where we have only sanitized it; we must remember that poetry is, in the ultimate sense, a secretion from within.

I think immediately of the best poetry of the late Allen Ginsberg. I think of lines by Stephen Dunn in "Middle Class Poem":

> Those with whom we sleep, never equally,
> roll away from us and sigh.

> When we wake
> the news of the world embraces us,
> pulls back. Who let go first?—
> a lover's question, the lover
> who's most alone.

I think of Adrienne Rich:

> I go down,
> My flippers cripple me,
> I crawl like an insect down the ladder
> and there is no one
> to tell me when the ocean
> will begin.

True poetry is rare. As Richard Howard suggests, it is subversive. When sitting in an airliner, I compulsively notice what my fellow passengers are reading. Rarely is it poetry. If it is, I feel an instant of . . . what? A bond with the reader? Not quite. It's almost as if the reader, male or female, were naked in broad daylight. There's something fishy about it, and I think of the book by Ray Bradbury, *Fahrenheit 451*, with its epigraph by Juan Ramon Jimenez:

> If they give you ruled paper,
> write the other way.

In the future society that Bradbury envisions, books are illegal. Members of the public fire department, instead of putting out fires, seek out caches of books which citizens have hidden and, with a flamethrower, torch them. The main character, Montag, is a member of the fire department. The citizens who read books have been forced to flee the city. To ensure the continuance of book culture, each of them has not only memorized a book. He has *become* a book.

In the climactic scene, Montag has wandered into the woods. One by one the books emerge from the trees and greet him:

> Granger touched Montag's arm. "Welcome back from the dead. . . . You might as well know all of us, now. This is Fred Clement, former occupant of the Thomas Hardy chair at Cambridge in the years before it became the Atomic Engineering School. This other is Dr. Simmons, from U.C.L.A., a specialist in Ortega y Gasset; . . . *We're* book burners, too. We read the books and burnt them, afraid they'd be found. Microfilming didn't pay off; we were always traveling, . . . Better to keep it in the old heads, where no one can see it or suspect it."

Bradbury wrote the book in 1950, at the height of the communist witch hunts and Sen. Joseph McCarthy's rule. The book is as urgently relevant today as it was in 1950. Or, as Richard Hugo wrote in his "Letter to Gale from Ovando":

> Roethke himself knew and hated to know the lonely roads
> we take to poems. Miriam Patchen was right in her speech
> in Portland: it's a one man route and sad. No help. No friend
> along the way, standing beside the road with trillium.

This is the road of people who read poetry. The road is marginal, as it should be, a road less traveled.

The reader returns home from a day in the office. Silence waits at the door. Inside, a book is waiting, like a bottle of fresh milk.

Index